The "No Experience" Job Search: Strategy and Workbook

The "No Experience" Job Search:

Strategy and Workbook

Written by, Kat McKay, J.D.

Published by MCKAY PUBLISHING

MCKAY PUBLISHING is located in Burlington Township, New Jersey 08016 USA.

MCKAY PUBLISHING is an independent publishing business associated with MCKAY RESEARCH, a textbook business located in Burlington Township, New Jersey 08016 USA. MCKAY PUBLISHING publishes educational books.

This book is for sale in nine countries upon its first edition publication.

TABLE OF CONTENTS

CHAPTER # 1

AN OVERVIEW OF THE STRATEGY

We sometimes think that one cannot get a job without having experience and cannot get experience without having a job. This guidebook will show you how to get a job by writing a resume that showcases either: (1) your skills (rather than your experience); or (2) a single experience or a few experiences (rather than prior positions). You will prepare to get the job you want, without having to have already had the job you want. You will remove yourself from the job search conundrum by restructuring your resume and your job searches to show what you can do, rather than simply list the positions you have held.

This job search will be designed around a set of resumes, which you will build from a master list describing your skills or individual experiences. The book will also guide you on how to write an effective cover letter, avoid networking pitfalls, interview well, and minimize bad references by keeping those bad influences away from your future employer.

This book guides job searchers who are transitioning to better experiences by showing them how to showcase skills and single experiences for a better position. It also guides recent university graduates by showing them how to showcase coursework, instead of job experience, to get the job the first time around.

Many people will tell you that your resume is your chance to present your qualifications for every new job by delineating prior positions, and that your cover letter is your chance to tailor your experience and strengths to each particular new position. Instead of this clichéd approach, I have created a way to have three separate resumes, each tailored to show a set of skills or single experiences that are most often requested by employers in your field.

You will learn to create a master resume list of your skills and experiences (those things you have done once) and then separate it into several different resumes. This way, you will have approximately three resumes, each showing different skills or experiences. Then, you will choose the resume that you will use to apply based on the requested skills or experiences stated in a job post.

For example, an office manager will create three resumes, each showcasing different skills (or strengths), which she creates from a master list of her skills and/or experiences. One resume might showcase her skills managing employee benefits in a small business environment (listing other skills or experiences lower on the resume). She would use this to apply to positions for which the company seeks someone with experience managing benefits for a small business.

Another resume (the second of the set of three) would be used to apply to positions with companies that request experience managing employee scheduling. It would also include information related to other skills or experiences as well.

A third resume (the last of the set) would showcase different skills or experiences and can be used to apply to positions with companies that primarily seek those skills or experiences.

These three resumes are all created from a master resume list, which the office manager drafted first. Her master resume list delineates all of her skills and individual experiences that she believes are most needed by employers in her field. She has determined what employers need the most by reviewing several posts seeking applications from office managers. She created a paragraph on her master resume list, under each listed topic, explaining her skills in that area and her experiences (even a single experience can work well). She has also included her personal information (name, phone number, email address, and street address), educational credentials (schools, diplomas or degrees, and dates received), and a list of any prior employers on her master resume list.

Once this master resume list is perfected by her and thoroughly proofread, she has only to electronically copy and paste her personal information and several specific skills and/or experiences (which she picks from her master resume list for that specific resume) onto each specific resume template. She will also include a list of her educational credentials, and most relevant prior employers from her master list, and electronically copy and paste these onto each resume template as well.

Each specific resume now showcases different skills (also called strengths) and/or experiences (or a single experience) and each, is therefore, tailored to a type of position that seeks that particular set of skills and/or experience. She will create approximately three such resumes; each geared toward a different type of position she is seeking, for which the posts seek different skills.

Now, she has three tailored resumes, which are fully ready for use to apply for positions. Because she has three tailored resumes, she can send them to potential employers with a cover letter, and the cover letter is not doing all of the work. The potential employer has a resume from the job candidate that focuses more fully on the areas of skill and experience, which are described in the employer's job posting.

By creating a master resume list, our job seeker also has more substance to pull from to create a substantive body for a cover letter for the position. Our job seeker can also use the substance of her master resume list to structure her communications for networking and interviewing. She is prepared with a thorough understanding of her fit for the many aspects of the field in which she is job searching.

CHAPTER #2

RESUME WRITING

We sometimes think that one cannot get a job without having experience and cannot get experience without having a job. This chapter will show you how to get the job by writing a resume that showcases either your skills (rather than your experience) or single experiences (rather than your prior positions) to get the job you want. Part one discusses how to build resumes by showcasing specific skills, and part two explains how to build resumes based on single work experiences or experience gained through coursework.

In this chapter, I consider two different resume formats (one based on showcasing skills and one based on showcasing single experiences) that are highly effective for transitioning to better positions. I use varied types of professionals who are likely to have different types of education and experience from one another as examples. By using varied examples of job seeking professionals, I hope to display the strengths of each format as it relates to each different educational and work background. I also seek to show how to draft resume paragraphs showcasing skills and single experiences.

Resumes showcasing specific skills are applicable to jobseekers with little experience. These resumes show that you have worked in this capacity in one prior position or are prepared to show that you can do something that you have not done before.

Resumes showcasing single experiences are also good for those who have done something once (in or out of an office) or who are recent graduates. Recent graduates who have only coursework experience will see how to write a resume to get the job the first time around. We will use the coursework to substantiate the experience.

Of course, you can use both specific skills and single experiences on the same resume. So, feel free to pick and choose from both sections as you write your master resume list and your resumes. If you have done something once, have only coursework in your pocket, or know you can do something that you have not done yet, this book will work for you.

Part One:

Showcasing Specific Skills

The professional resume is an opportunity to showcase your accomplishments and to connect your work history or academic background with the needs of your potential employer. Once you have identified the "type of position" that you are seeking, then, locate some readily available job listings (such as those online or in a trade publication). Look at the jobs to which you would want to apply and decide if your "type of position" has some variation.

For example, a future secretary might wish to apply for a variety of types of secretarial positions, such as ones in a small business (with an additional requirement of acting as a receptionist and seeking telephone skills and typing), or legal secretarial positions (seeking proofreading and deadline tracking experience), or positions in a large company (seeking organization and promptness). This secretarial job seeker may choose to create three versions of her resume. The first to be used to apply to positions focused on typing and telephone communication, another designed to respond to law firm needs, and a third version to be sent to positions whose posts seek someone organized and prompt.

The best way to create these versions of a resume is to create a list of what you perceive to be the most necessary qualities in your field and to then categorize your skills under each listed heading. For example, a person who has done these things in one prior position might write:

Skillful Typing and Editing: I type (number of) words per minute. I regularly typed and edited documents for (person's name) and (person's name) while working for (business name) from (date) to (date). These documents most often included formal correspondence, lengthy reports of up to (number of) pages, and business agreements. I pride myself on rarely making errors. I regularly confirm with my supervisor any details that have been provided to me if they look inaccurate. I do this to ensure that the best possible work product is sent to business partners and to clients. I strive to be the most accurate person in the office.

Proficient Telephone Communications: I communicated with clients and prospective clients, business partners, and a variety of other callers, as part of my position with (business name), from (date) to (date). I have a professional demeanor in all interactions. I am kind and willing to help the caller find the person for whom they are calling or the proper person to answer their question. I always return messages promptly, and I will confirm the response as needed with my supervisor.

You may also use a skills-based resume without citing a prior position. You simply delete the first line, for example:

Skillful Typing and Editing: I type (number of) words per minute. I am skilled at typing and editing documents. These documents include formal correspondence, lengthy reports, and business agreements. I pride myself on rarely making errors. I will regularly confirm with my supervisor any details which have been provided to me if they look inaccurate. I will do this to ensure that the best possible work product is sent to business partners and to clients. I strive to be the most accurate person in the office.

Proficient Telephone Communications: I will communicate well with clients and prospective clients, business partners, and a variety of other callers. I have a professional demeanor in all interactions. I am kind and willing to help any caller find the person for whom they are calling or the proper person to answer their question. I always return messages promptly, and I will confirm the response as needed with my supervisor.

Keep in mind that you can mix paragraphs showing what you have done with those showing what you can do. Next, when you have a full list of the necessary skills and best explanations of how you exemplify them, you will add the remaining resume components to the master list. These often include your educational background and a list of relevant positions that you have held, the dates of your work in those positions, and the businesses for which you held those positions. Make sure you honestly communicate what you have done, plus what you know you can do.

You now have a master list of information that you can use to build various versions of your resume to respond to specific job leads and postings of positions. Carefully proofread it and have two others carefully proofread it as well. Then, electronically copy and paste it into three resume formats that you wish to create. Choose how to arrange each resume by putting the necessary strengths for that type of post first. You might end up with the same information organized in three different ways (each with a different top skill). Or, you may choose to only list the primarily needed skills for a given position type; leaving the other skills, which are not as necessary for that type of position, off of that resume format. Your choice might depend on how many skills you have, or the depth of expertise that you have in each skill on your list.

Once you are happy with each resume version proofread them again for errors, especially spacing and formatting errors (which could be made when electronically copying and pasting paragraphs from your master list). Now, you have three versions of your resume, each of which showcases different skills. You can choose the resume that most closely corresponds to a given position and provide that version when you apply for that position.

Notably, a resume showcasing specific skills could be used for almost any type of work. An office manager who wishes to showcase her skills might include the following skills on her master list: organizational skills, ability to manage staff, ability to manage an office budget, ability to properly coordinate the purchasing needs for the office, knowledge of specific computer software needed to perform these tasks, and an understanding of how to manage employee benefits for a small business.

Then, she should create a paragraph under each necessary skill that she has identified as pertaining to the jobs to which she will likely apply. She will want to match her skills to the needs identified in the job postings that she has seen and that appeal to her. She will take the skills identified in the posting and ask herself how her background has already provided her with some depth in that area and what she knows she can do. Then, she will draft a paragraph for each such skill demonstrating her depth of understanding and knowledge. Here are some examples of ways that she could explain her work experience based on one prior position:

Practiced Manager of Office Staff: While working for (business) from (date) to (date), I worked closely with the business owner and fulfilled her needs by responsibly managing the eight employees in the (location) office. I oversaw scheduling, answered and facilitated employees in obtaining answers to questions related to health insurance and other benefits, and communicated the owner's needs to those in our office as instructed. The owner of this business has two office locations, and I enabled her to spend her time at the other location by properly managing the office.

Skilled at Budgeting and Coordinating Office Purchases: I have had significant responsibility coordinating the purchases of office supplies for an office. In a prior position, the office employed five employees who performed a variety of tasks. Ensuring the supplies needed by each employee were on hand involved developing an understanding of the mechanics of each employee's role and how it was carried out. It also required excellent budgeting and properly timing the orders to meet the needs of office employees. I succeeded in coordinating office purchases, including obtaining the correct supplies, with excellent timing and proper budgeting.

Here is a way that concentrates only on the skill itself and no prior position. Our future office manager demonstrates what she can do:

Adept at Managing Office Staff: I am able to oversee scheduling, answer and facilitate employees in obtaining answers to questions related to health insurance and other benefits, and communicate an owner's needs to those in the office as instructed. I am organized, skillful, and good with people.

Skilled at Budgeting and Coordinating Office Purchases: I am able to coordinate the purchases of office supplies for an office. I will ensure the supplies needed by each employee are on hand, and I can develop an understanding of the supplies and ordering, which is needed for an office. I also have the skills to budget and properly time the orders to meet the needs of office employees. I am able to coordinate the needs of an office; including office purchases and the proper timing and budgeting associated with those purchases.

Notably, the previous paragraph provides an example of a way to easily discuss skills which you have, but which you have not done yet in a position. You can also use this type of format to describe a single position without providing the specifics of the position in the paragraph. If you choose to discuss skills that you have gained without naming the specific businesses in which you learned them, simply include a full list of your relevant employers elsewhere on your resume. Be prepared to explain very honestly the reasons that you know you can do this skill well and why you should be hired based on what you can do, not what you have done.

You will create your master list of skills, and include on it a list of positions and employers (most often with dates of your employment), and a synopsis of your educational background. Then, you can carefully check your work (as well as having two others proofread it as well), and create the three resume format which you will then use to respond to the several different types of positions that you have seen and which interest you.

Examples of three different posts for office manager positions could be: (1) those stressing skills regarding scheduling staff; (2) those requiring detailed knowledge relating to the particular line of work of the business; and (3) those requiring knowledge of managing employee benefits in a small office environment.

A resume showcasing specific skills could also work well for many other professionals. For example, an attorney's master resume list could include trial advocacy skills and motion argument experience (even "moot court" experience gained in law school), as well as research and writing work (possibly from writing school papers). Then, the attorney could create three resumes and have a resume ready to apply to positions requiring mostly research and written work, a different resume for a position requiring strong motion argument skills, and a resume for positions aimed at settling cases. Paragraphs for the research and written work resume version might look like this (notably, these are created without citing a prior position):

> **Skilled Researcher:** Litigation often centers on accurate research. I have significant skill researching complex legal issues in all 50 states; and researching contracts, their provisions, and the laws relating to them.

> **Aggressive Writer:** Litigation often requires detailed and aggressive writing. I have significant skill drafting litigation documents, including: legal briefs asserting persuasive arguments; detailed memoranda summarizing case law relevant to client issues; discovery motions and motions for summary judgment; case evaluations for clients delineating case strategy, factual and legal analysis, and proposed resolutions; pleadings; interrogatories and requests for production of documents; and legal correspondence to clients and opposing counsel.

Notably, a skills-based resume blends what you have done with what you can do. Be honest, and prepare to explain why you know that you can do it! For example, a recent law school graduate might say "I know I am skilled in arguing, because I won the 'moot court' competition in law school. While I have not had a chance to do it for a client, I am excellent at it."

Building several resumes, each of which showcases specific skills which you have and that are applicable to different types of positions to which you will most likely apply is smart. Any resume is about showcasing your skills and experience and matching it to available positions that you would want to have. Having several versions of a resume, each with different skills showcased, enables you to send it off quickly in response to many more posts or leads. Just send the one that most closely matches the job post or job lead. Then, you have aligned your skills more closely to the skills that the employer has described as necessary for the position. When the skills you explain on your resume more closely match the needs of the position, then you are more likely to get the job.

Part Two:

Highlighting Specific Examples of Your Work

A second type of resume that you might choose is a resume highlighting specific examples of your work. A specific example of your work does not have to be a large project that you headed up for many months. It could be a relatively small experience that demonstrates something that you do well. Using an example is a way to make a small project (or the time that you pitched in and did your former boss's project) into an experience that can demonstrate a skill that you need (and that you have) for a better job. If you have done it even once, then you can use it as an example of your past work. I will also show how coursework provides excellent examples for recent graduates to use.

Let us consider how to build a list of good examples. We can consider a receptionist who would rather apply for a secretarial position this time around. Our receptionist will have many telephone and in-person communication skills and experiences that he can showcase. But, what if he has had limited letter writing and proofreading experience? Well, he is good at these tasks and is certain that he will do an excellent job. One way to provide a resume that honestly shows his written communication work experience is to provide an example of a time that he worked with others providing overflow secretarial support for his prior office.

Even if this duty was only handled by the receptionist once or twice for a few hours, he can use this as an example on his resume. He would do well to create an example of a specific experience on the particularly busy overflow day, where he prepared letters for a company executive or business owner. His master resume list might include a simple list of ten or so work skills and then contain descriptive examples of each. His example of written communication work might read:

Written Communication Experience: I have experience writing and editing letters. For example, I once assisted the (company name) Vice President of Purchasing in writing and sending important correspondence to a major supplier after work hours. I stayed late to help the Vice President of Purchasing when his secretary was unavailable. I also assisted two other (company name) executives by helping to draft and/or edit their written communications. Because of this, I know I am adaptable to different styles of writing and to helping draft correspondence that is both articulate and efficient.

The same receptionist may have a bit of experience assisting in organizing the office filing system to create office space for an incoming new hire. He might have had a long conversation with the office manager and a few secretaries as they debated where to put the files. He may add this to his example list to demonstrate that he is capable of file organization on a larger scale in his next position. He might write the following example:

> **Experience Managing File Organization:** I am able to organize and manage files. For example, I was a central participant in a project relocating an entire file room. As a part of this experience, I participated in a discussion of the organizational strategy used for the filing system. This included, strategy relating to immediate accessibility needs of particular professionals' files, off-site file storage options for dated files, and problems with the methods used in the current organizational system. I helped to delineate a new strategy and implemented it to successful completion.

Listing detailed examples of projects is a great way to show that you are good at doing something that you have not been given a significant chance to do yet, but which you have a bit of experience doing. Using a resume structured from specific examples can help you to beat the unrealistic but real problem that you need experience to get the job, and you need the job to get experience.

We switch positions to better ones (we hope) and job posts for those better positions seek better experience. Try to show that you have some of this necessary experience through specific examples of the work that you have done. If you have done it even once, then you have an example!

No one knows this better than a recent college graduate. Let us presume that our college graduate has worked on campus part-time shelving books in the library and over the summers in a restaurant waiting tables. Our recent college graduate is, of course, educated and wishes for a more advanced position.

Our graduate applies for a position in his chosen field, which is business. He hopes to gain some "real world" experience before returning to school later for a Master of Business Administration degree (MBA). Our college graduate wishes to primarily apply to small businesses in which he hopes that he can learn the inner workings of many parts of the business. Someday, he thinks that he might open a business on his own. He has found several leads and postings for small businesses needing employees of various types. His strategy (he has decided) will be to send lots of resumes and hopefully obtain a number of interviews. Then he hopes to be able to choose a position which will allow him to participate in many aspects of the business. He believes that this will provide him with some understanding of how to run a small business and whether he thinks he will be suited to it.

Our college graduate is most attracted to possibly owning an independent or large franchise bookstore later on. He is also possibly interested in owning a franchise educational center (such as a tutoring center) or a franchise test preparation center (for example, one that prepares students to take graduate entrance exams).

After identifying potential postings and leads, he might consider building a master resume list based on specific examples of his work experience. This will highlight his more relevant experiences while minimizing hours spent monotonously shelving books and carrying sandwiches. He identifies the following qualities to accentuate: organization of book filing systems, knowledge of authors and book content, working directly with customers, operating a cash register (and accepting coupons), and resolving disputed prices. He also might list time spent tutoring a student to whom he provided assistance. From this list, he will build a list of examples of his work (each in paragraph form) and then, choose how to format them into several versions of a resume. Each resume is geared to a different business owner from whom he hopes to obtain a position. Remember, our college graduate does not only want to run the cash register; he wants a job learning to run the whole store because some day he will own one.

Keep in mind, that if our college graduate had a different goal, such as to work as a librarian and consider getting a Master of Library and Information Science (MLIS); in a museum (potentially cataloging exhibit information); or in a law firm and consider going to law school to obtain a Juris Doctor (JD); then, paragraphs developed from this list could also work for those applications. These and more can be built from our graduate's jobs waiting tables and shelving books in the library:

- o Book organization
- o Decision-making regarding filing systems for books
- o Knowledge of authors and book content
- o Building customer relationships

- o Money transactions (including following financial guidelines, keeping proper records, accepting coupons, operating a cash register and credit card device)
- o Resolving disputes (such as price disputes)

Now, let us use another example: a college graduate who would like to immediately enter a field which she studied in college. This college graduate studied marketing. Her specific major was food marketing. In college, she learned how major food companies market their foods in grocery stores (such as Kraft Foods and Nabisco). She has studied and not worked while in college. She can build an example-based resume focusing on and describing examples of her coursework. She has a degree in the field of food marketing, and she created several projects (of which she is proud) during her time in college. These projects, her coursework, and tests will provide the material for a resume based on examples. She can use them to highlight her relevant knowledge and experience working through important issues in food marketing.

Our college graduate finds posts and positions to which she would like to apply and reviews them. She creates a list of the experience sought by several potential employers. Then, she fits her coursework, course projects, and group experiences into the categories, which she has listed to provide the examples. She demonstrates the needed experience through well-written examples, which discuss the experience that she has gained in school.

Let us presume that our college graduate has listed the following experiences as being sought by potential employers in postings for positions for which she would like to apply. The employer seeks an employee with experience using a specific type of spreadsheet format and software to understand sales overtime and to input sales data; understanding a variety of prominent methods to display foods in stores to increase sales; and restructuring in store product quantities at times of high-volume sales to focus on season-specific products.

Our college graduate, who was introduced to the applicable spreadsheet format in class, became familiar with it, and was tested on it (along with other course topics), so she might write:

Demonstrated Knowledge of (Named) Spreadsheet Format and Software Used to Create It:

Knowledge: I am thoroughly familiar with the (named) spreadsheet format. I have studied this format including its usual applicability in four situations, including: (1) first situation she studied; (2) second situation she studied; (3) third situation she studied; and (4) fourth situation she studied.

Testing: I successfully demonstrated my understanding of when and how to use these spreadsheets through a testing process. I scored a (percentage correct) on the questions related to these spreadsheets.

Practical Application: I am familiar with the most recent uses of this spreadsheet. I used (named) software to create a spreadsheet to delineate food purchasing changes over Thanksgiving weekend, and I, therefore, have demonstrated practical knowledge and application of this software by using it to create a readable spreadsheet in the relevant field.

Notably, our recent college graduate used the software (delineating purchasing changes over Thanksgiving weekend) as a class project or to fulfill a class assignment. She has the experience necessary to create the example although she has never before had a job.

Demonstrated Understanding of Prominent Methods for Large Scale Grocery Store Displays:

Display Planning: I have demonstrated my knowledge of prominent methods used for large scale displays in grocery stores. I have studied large scale grocery store displays, and I have implemented this knowledge by creating a presentation that is ready to present to a marketing group, recommending that a large scale display of (name of product, such as Kraft salad dressings) be changed to encourage purchasing of (name of specific product, such as Kraft ranch salad dressing) during the summer season. I presented this idea to my peers and two professionals (names of professionals or professors) in the field and received a significantly positive response. This demonstrated knowledge is current and shows my understanding of the field of food marketing.

Document Creation Related to Display Planning: I created a set of documents related to this presentation of my proposed display plan using (name of format). By creating these and other similar documents, I have also demonstrated my capable knowledge of these formats and that I have the necessary knowledge to support group work in a company environment.

Knowledge of How to Change Product Quantities to Focus on Season-Specific Products During Times of High-Volume Sales:

Knowledge of Product Quantity Changes: I reviewed product quantities at times of low volume and high-volume purchasing and considered how to encourage sales of season-specific products, while maintaining sufficient stock of low volume products. I balanced the increased purchasing of the seasonal products with continued purchasing of low volume products and worked through ideas of how these products can be shelved. Additional issues included limited shelf space, expiration dates, and the quick fall-off of purchases of seasonal products after specific holidays. I met with a group to discuss these issues on a regular basis.

Notably, for the third example, I presumed that our recent college graduate has not created an entire project focused on the shelf-stocking issue but that she has consistently considered this issue in her food marketing courses and in her study groups, or as a part of projects with related goals. She has seen that this is a repeated portion of the job postings that she has found, so she has used her coursework and studies in this area as her example.

While it may seem that creating a specific example from general coursework and studies would be difficult, as I have shown here, it certainly can be done. Our college graduate has spent four years studying marketing. This is certainly a significant amount of time spent gaining knowledge and demonstrating her understanding. This work provides excellent substance for an example-based resume.

On the interview, our college graduate should prepare to discuss her examples with some additional depth. She should also prepare to explain the significance of her knowledge base and her ability to practically apply it to business pursuits. She can state with enthusiasm how current and deep her knowledge is and her readiness to transition into application in a food company and/or store environment.

Part Three:

Explaining that Coursework is Experience to a Potential Employer

It is important to be an enthusiastic proponent of your experience. If you are met with skepticism, such as a truculent interviewer's statements of "I am not sure that coursework is applicable work experience. I am used to reading about actual work experience on a resume." Then, politely and happily state that you are very much looking forward to new experiences in a company environment and that you have a significant amount of current knowledge to offer.

I recommend that you do not directly argue in an interview setting about the validity of applying coursework examples in the place of the interviewers' regularly seen (and more basic) entry-level position experiences. Instead, positively and charismatically reiterate your excitement to work in a company environment and that you have a significant amount of knowledge gained from the coursework and projects. Communicate that you are seeking this opportunity because you will be good at it. Further, that you know that you will be good at it because you have the understanding and knowledge that the position needs as demonstrated by your coursework, excellent grades, and resulting degree.

Remember, you are overcoming the tricky issue of needing experience to get the job and the job to get experience. Never let an interview turn into an argument of whether coursework experience is exactly right. Almost no prior experience is exactly right for every position. Just discuss the qualities that make you a good fit (even if you have to dodge the question a bit). Respond to a question that implies your coursework is insufficient by stating that you have current knowledge in the field (shown by your degree and major); are a high-level thinker (shown by your grade point average, school attended, and completion of a bachelor's degree); dress appropriately; arrive promptly; are great to work with; and put the needed time and effort into each project. These qualities are certainly applicable to the position. Plus, your resume was selected for an interview, showing that your coursework experience has already been well received by some in the company.

We can use these same methods to create example-based resume formats for liberal arts students applying to work in their fields. Liberal arts students have a variety of majors and consider varied fields upon graduation. A pre-law major (or English, history, philosophy, or other major) who wants to enter the legal field, may want to work as a paralegal. Most often, this graduate would obtain a paralegal certification first. Or, he may want to work in the field for a year or two in another capacity and then apply to law school.

If he pursues the route of paralegal certification, he would use an example-based format that is very similar to the food marketing graduate. He would list coursework and certificate completion as the substance of his qualifications. He would identify from postings, the main qualifications for entry-level paralegal positions, and create paragraphs demonstrating his knowledge and understanding in each area through an example. His resume paragraphs might highlight his understanding of:

o Reading difficult texts
o Culling factual information
o Using facts found to support arguments in written work
o Excellent decision-making when considering how to use detailed information
o Detail-oriented writing skills
o Ability to persuade
o Willingness to organize files, review transcripts, and write basic or detailed correspondence

Established professionals may want to use their work experience to teach university or other courses. However, they may have trouble obtaining teaching positions without the specific type of experience the educational institution seeks. An attorney who wishes to teach courses may, for example, create a course and market it to a provider of continuing legal education courses for attorneys. This would entail researching and writing the course materials, and then sending them to organizations who might hire the attorney to teach the course. He may then use these courses taught to apply to teach individual courses at the law school level. This is a way of building experience from the ground up. He markets something he has never taught to show he can, and then uses those successes to market himself further to higher-level course providers (such as actual law schools).

Established professionals may also consider taking on group projects (such as work on group publications or work as a group on a large-scale project) to show that the professional has the capacity to do this work on his or her own. Again, experience is built from the ground up, so we simply characterize what we have (be it coursework, a single experience, or a skill) to convince someone that we are ready for the position we want. Then we use that to build experience for the next position, and again re-characterize our experience to take the leap for which we are ready (but despite our readiness, for which we do not yet have any depth of experience; we only have limited experience).

Part Four:

Resume Examples

Here is an example resume. Notice that this is a new professional, and he has done many of these tasks exactly once. He states them in a big way, while maintaining complete honesty:

Name, Esq.
Email Address
Phone Number
Address

EDUCATION

J.D., month and year, Name of University School of Law
Class rank
Accolade received
Law school TA position held

B.A., month and year, Name of University School of Law
Class rank
Accolade received

BAR ADMISSIONS

Name of State of Admission
United States District Court for the District of State

ATTORNEY ACCOMPLISHMENTS

I am a new law school graduate and I am skilled in the areas in which associate attorneys need to excel.

Litigation often centers on accurate, detailed, and aggressive communication. I am a successful arguer and I understand the need for accuracy and zeal. I have experience doing each of the following:

- Arguing a motion for summary judgment;
- Conducting two discovery depositions;
- Appearing in court for eight necessary conferences;

- Conducting a client interview and preparing the client for a court appearance;
- Advising two clients of the law and communicating potential legal arguments; and
- Negotiating three settlements.

I am an excellent researcher and writer, and can:
- Research complex legal issues in all 50 states;
- Research contracts, their provisions, and the laws relating to them;
- Draft litigation documents, including: legal briefs asserting persuasive arguments; detailed memoranda summarizing case law relevant to client issues; discovery motions and motions for summary judgment; case evaluations for clients delineating case strategy, factual and legal analysis, and proposed resolutions; pleadings; interrogatories and requests for production of documents; and legal correspondence to clients and opposing counsel.

HISTORY OF POSITIONS HELD

The full list of positions from which I have gained this work experience are as follows (in order of the significance of the position to my work experience):

Law firm (date to date)

Law student teacher's assistant (date to date)

Here is a second example resume, for our secretarial job seeker from above:

Name
Email Address
Phone Number
Address

EDUCATION
School attended and degree or diploma received, date received

RELEVANT TESTING AND SOFTWARE KNOWLEDGE
Typing test, with a speed of (number of) words per minute
Microsoft Excel
Microsoft Word
Power Point

SECRETARIAL ACCOMPLISHMENTS
Written Communication Experience: I have experience writing and editing letters. For example, I assisted the (company name) Vice President of Purchasing in writing and sending important correspondence to a major supplier after hours. I stayed late to help the Vice President of Purchasing when his secretary was unavailable. I also assisted at least five other (company name) executives by helping to draft and/or edit their written communications on a regular basis. Because of this, I am adaptable to different styles of writing and to helping draft correspondence that is both articulate and efficient.

Experience Managing File Organization: I am able to organize and manage files. For example, I was a central participant in a project relocating an entire file room. As a part of this experience, I participated in a discussion of the organizational strategy used for the filing system. This included strategy relating to immediate accessibility needs of particular professionals' files, off-site file storage options for dated files, and problems with the methods used in the current organizational system. I helped to delineate a new strategy and implemented it to successful completion.

Proficient Telephone Communications: I will communicate well with clients and prospective clients, business partners, and a variety of other callers. I have a professional demeanor in all interactions. I am kind and willing to help any caller find the person for whom they are calling or the proper person to answer their question. I always return messages promptly, and I will confirm the response as needed with my supervisor.

LIST OF RELEVANT POSITIONS HELD

Position type, business, from date to date
Position type, business, from date to date

Here is a third example resume, for our recent food marketing graduate who has not yet had a job, but has coursework to showcase:

Name
Email Address
Phone Number
Address

EDUCATION
School attended, degree received, date received
Class rank
Accolades

RELEVANT SOFTWARE KNOWLEDGE
Name of software
Name of software
Name of software

RELEVANT INDUSTRY SKILLS
Demonstrated Knowledge of (Named) Spreadsheet Format and Software Used to Create It:
- **Knowledge:** I am thoroughly familiar with the (named) spreadsheet format. I have studied this format including its usual applicability in four situations, including: (1) first situation she studied; (2) second situation she studied; (3) third situation she studied; and (4) fourth situation she studied.
- **Testing:** I successfully demonstrated my understanding of when and how to use these spreadsheets through a testing process. I scored a (percentage correct) on the questions related to these spreadsheets.
- **Practical Application:** I am familiar with the most recent uses of this spreadsheet. I used (named) software to create a spreadsheet to delineate food purchasing changes over Thanksgiving weekend and I, therefore, have demonstrated practical knowledge and application of this software by using it to create a readable spreadsheet in the relevant field.

Demonstrated Understanding of Prominent Methods for Large-Scale Grocery Store Displays:

- **Display Planning:** I have demonstrated my knowledge of prominent methods used for large-scale displays in grocery stores. I have studied large-scale grocery store displays, and I have implemented this knowledge by creating a presentation, which is ready to present to a marketing group, recommending that a large-scale display of (name of product, such as Kraft salad dressings) be changed to encourage purchasing of (name of specific product, such as Kraft ranch salad dressing) during the summer season. I presented this idea to my peers and two professionals (names of professionals or professors) in the field and received a significantly positive response. This demonstrated knowledge is current and shows my understanding of the field of food marketing.
- **Document Creation Related to Display Planning:** I created a set of documents related to this presentation of my proposed display plan using (name of format). By creating these and other similar documents, I have also demonstrated my capable knowledge of these formats and that I have the necessary knowledge to support group work in a company environment.

Knowledge of How to Change Product Quantities to Focus on Season-Specific Products, During Times of High-Volume Sales:
- **Knowledge of Product Quantity Changes:** I reviewed product quantities at times of low volume and high volume purchasing and considered how to encourage sales of season- specific products, while maintaining sufficient stock of low-volume products. I balanced the increased purchasing of the seasonal products with continued purchasing of low-volume products and worked through ideas of how these products can be shelved. Additional issues included limited shelf space, expiration dates, and the quick fall-off of purchases of seasonal products after specific holidays. I met with a group to discuss these issues on a regular basis.

Here is a fourth example resume for our office manager jobseeker from above:

Name
Email Address
Phone Number
Address

EDUCATION
School attended and degree or diploma received, date received

RELEVANT SOFTWARE KNOWLEDGE
Microsoft Excel
Microsoft Word
Power Point

SKILLS AND EXPERIENCE
Adept at Managing Office Staff: I am able to oversee scheduling, answer and facilitate employees in obtaining answers to questions related to health insurance and other benefits, and communicate an owner's needs to those in the office as instructed. I am organized, skillful, and good with people.

Skilled at Budgeting and Coordinating Office Purchases: I am able to coordinate the purchases of office supplies for an office. I will ensure the supplies needed by each employee are on hand, and I can develop an understanding of the supplies and ordering that is needed for an office. I also have the skills to budget and properly time the orders to meet the needs of office employees. I am able to coordinate the needs of an office including office purchases and the proper timing and budgeting associated with those purchases.

Experience Managing File Organization: I am able to organize and manage files. For example, I was a central participant in a project relocating an entire file room. As a part of this experience, I participated in a discussion of the organizational strategy used for the filing system. This included strategy relating to immediate accessibility needs of particular professionals' files, off-site file storage options for dated files, and problems with the methods used in the current organizational system. I helped to delineate a new strategy and implemented it to successful completion.

Written Communication Experience: I have experience writing and editing letters. For example, I assisted the (company name) Vice President of Purchasing in writing and sending important correspondence to a major supplier after hours. I stayed late to help the Vice President of Purchasing when his secretary was unavailable. I also assisted at least five other (company name) executives by helping to draft and/or edit their written communications on a regular basis. Because of this, I am adaptable to different styles of writing and to helping draft correspondence that is both articulate and efficient.

LIST OF RELEVANT POSITIONS HELD
Position type, business, from date to date
Position type, business, from date to date

CHAPTER #**3**

UPDATING LINKEDIN TO MAKE CONNECTIONS ELECTRONICALLY

After your resumes are created, you will want an "online presence." At this point, you will have approximately three resumes showcasing different strengths or experiences for positions in the same field. These will better match different employers' specific needs in that field. You will have created these resumes from your initial master resume list. You can create an excellent LinkedIn profile in a very short time by electronically copying and pasting your strengths and experiences, your educational credentials, and your work history (a simple list of any positions held and dates) from your master resume list onto your new LinkedIn profile.

You can categorize the information under each position you held or play with the site to create your own structure. For example, if you teach classes as part of various positions or without a steady employer for this teaching, and your master resume list lists experience teaching courses as a category of experience, then play with ways to include this same format on LinkedIn. Potentially title the header "Course Teaching" and use a date range from the first course you taught to the current day. Then the body of that section could list the courses and the substance of those courses as it is listed on your master resume list.

I recommend that you include all of your experiences and strengths as they are formatted on your resumes, but you will have to play with the site (as per the prior teaching example) to do this. Once your master resume list and corresponding two or three resumes have been created and proofread, then you have all of the needed information to create a significantly detailed and comprehensive LinkedIn profile. It will not take you long because you will be able to electronically copy and paste the exact work that you have already done to create your master resume list and resulting resumes.

Electronically copying and pasting each experience, skill, and position, as well as all of your educational credentials (everything from your master resume list), will create a more significant LinkedIn profile than any single resume that you have created. This is because it contains the components of all of your resume materials. Add a picture that displays you in a professional manner and you are finished. It is always helpful to ask another person to double check for any errors or typos accidentally created by your electronic copying and pasting.

Next, scout out connections and be liberal in sending connection requests to people you know and those with whom you have worked. Having a significant LinkedIn profile can help others to see your qualifications in full, without your having to directly email them. If you meet someone to whom you would wish to provide your professional information, then you can send them a connection request. This will also help you to keep track of their name and where they work without too much organizing or memory on your part. A follow-up email to their work account with one of your resume versions is also a good idea.

CHAPTER #4

COVER LETTERS

Part One:

Cover Letter Basics

To create a cover letter, first create a template that is formatted as a professional business letter. Then, draft an initial letter by using information from your master resume list to form much of the body of your letter. Next, for each cover letter you write, switch some of the information you include to better match the job description. My recommendation is to switch as little as possible each time you create the cover letter. You might be able to switch only the recipient's name, address, date, name of the company, and name of the position for which you are applying.

The most significant pitfall in writing cover letters is accidentally including typographical errors. When you switch more information more often, you may have trouble keeping typos out of your cover letters. Therefore, you should consider whether this is a likely problem for you. If it is, then switch less and keep the body of the letter primarily intact. If it is not, then consider switching more information in each letter to more fully match it to each job description.

To switch less information, create a substantial one page letter that contains several strengths or highlights a few points of your experiences, which you believe will be the most applicable to many potential jobs to which you may apply. Then, create a very short initial paragraph immediately after the salutation ("Dear Mr. _____") which states the position to which you are applying, where you found the post or learned of the position, and a single sentence regarding your qualifications for this particular position.

This two-sentence opener is then the only portion that you will need to revise (in addition to the address, date, and recipient's name) for every letter to tailor it in a very simple way to the position. This can help you to avoid typographical errors in your cover letters, tailor them sufficiently to the position, and prepare them quickly.

Your three resumes are more tailored to the position description, and you will save time now that the two main pieces of your job search portfolio (the resume and cover letter) are created. The extra time that you spent to create two or three resumes directed more fully toward different job descriptions will be saved later as you quickly apply to positions with readily directed resumes and easily tailored cover letters.

Part Two:

A Strategy Refresher

Remember our initial strategy from Chapter One. Many people will tell you that your resume is your chance to present your qualifications for every new job by delineating prior positions and that your cover letter is your chance to tailor your experience and strengths to each particular new position. Instead of this exhausted approach, our strategy is to create approximately three separate resumes, each tailored to show a set of skills or experiences that are most often requested by employers in your field. Each resume is more closely tailored to a type of qualification employers seek. So, you send the resume that most closely matches an employer's post. We did this by creating a master resume list of your skills and experiences (even things you have done once) and then separating it into several different resumes.

As you recall, our example jobseekers in Chapter Two determined what employers need the most by reviewing several posts seeking applications in their fields. They then each created paragraphs for a master resume list, and under each listed topic explained their skills in that area and their experiences (we saw how even a single experience can work well). Our example jobseekers also included their educational credentials and a list of prior employers on their master resume lists.

Once this master resume list was perfected, and thoroughly proofread, each example jobseeker had only to electronically copy and paste his or her personal information (name, phone number, email address, and street address), and several specific skills and/or experiences (which each picked from his or her master resume list) onto each specific resume template. Each example jobseeker also included a list of his or her educational credentials, and most relevant prior employers on their master lists and electronically copied and pasted these onto each resume template as well.

Each specific resume they created showcased different skills (also called strengths) and/or experiences (or a single experience) and each was therefore, tailored to a type of position that sought that particular set of skills and/or experiences.

Now, the job of the cover letter is lessened. This is because once you create three tailored resumes (like our example jobseeker), you can send them to potential employers with a cover letter, and the cover letter is not doing all of the work. The potential employer has a resume from you, which focuses more fully on the areas of skill and experience that are described in the employer's job posting.

You have also created more substance to pull from to use to create a substantive body for your cover letter for the position. You can also use the substance of your master resume list to structure your communications for networking and interviewing. Finally, you are prepared with a thorough understanding of your fit for the many aspects of the field in which you are job searching.

Part Three:

How the Cover Letter Fits Into the Strategy

Because you have three tailored resumes, your cover letter is not doing all of the work. Your resume focuses more directly on showcasing your qualifications for the position that you are seeking. Remember that many other job seekers' resumes primarily delineate prior positions held (which we term experience), rather than their direct qualifications (skills and individual experiences) for this specific position.

Because you have created a master resume list and three resumes, now your cover letter can also have more substance. You can choose to copy and paste portions of your master list into the body of your cover letter. Portions of your cover letter can match a piece of the resume that you send with the letter.

You can do this because some employers tend to read cover letters and some do not. Therefore, it is a good idea to have a few finished resumes that are each targeted more closely to the position, since your cover letter may not be read. Furthermore, your cover letter may not make it past the intake person in human resources, while your resume will more likely be sent to the person in the company for whom you may directly work. You want your cover letter to be well written and sufficiently substantive to convince human resources or another intake person to send your resume on to the decision-maker. If you send it directly to the decision-maker, you want it to be good. However, because you know it is not always read by (and sometimes not even forwarded to) the decision-maker, we should concentrate most fully on the targeted resume.

While a targeted resume is of primary importance, a substantive cover letter (about one page including addresses, date, salutation, and signature line) that you create from substance you already drafted for you master resume list is still needed. Remember that the most significant pitfall in writing cover letters is to accidentally include typographical errors. Therefore, you may also want to create a few example cover letters and switch as little as possible each time you send one out.

Draft a very short initial paragraph immediately after the salutation ("Dear Mr. _____") that states the position to which you are applying, where you found the post or learned of the position, and a single sentence regarding your qualifications for this particular position. Then, this two-sentence opener is the only portion that you will need to revise (along with the address, date, and recipient's name) for every letter to tailor it in a very simple way to the position. This can help you to avoid typographical errors in your cover letters, tailor them sufficiently to the position, and prepare them quickly.

Part Four:

Example Cover Letters

Here is a cover letter that a new graduate might use to apply to coordinate a program on a university campus:

Name
Address
Telephone Number
Email Address

Date

Recipient's Name
Recipient's Address

Dear University Scholarship Program,

I am applying for the position of University Scholarship Program Coordinator at Name of University. I found a post stating that you are currently seeking to fill this position with a qualified applicant.

I am a Name of University graduate and I am committed to education. I would love to work with and coordinate the program for students who are continuing in education by seeking scholarship funding. I am very interested in student achievement, and I am a significantly motivational person for those who are continually "gaining speed" in their academic achievements.

I currently teach standardized examination preparation to students preparing to enroll in college for Name of Tutoring Center in Town, State. I teach examination preparation to students who at times have trouble with the ACT or SAT, and who are looking to improve academically as students. They are on the verge of entering college and are also "gaining speed" academically. I feel that I develop good relationships with the students, and I connect well with them. I am encouraged by their progress, and I would love to work to coordinate a program that will help others emerge as scholars by obtaining scholarship resources.

I am interested in working as a University Scholarship Program Coordinator at Name of University, and I am certainly able to fulfill the administrative and coordination needs of your office. I find this posted position to be consistent with both my background and my interests. I hope that you will find my qualifications applicable and consider me for this position.

Sincerely,

Job Seeker

Job Seeker

Here is another example cover letter which is different in substance:

Name
Address
Telephone Number
Email Address

Date

Recipient's Name
Recipient's Address

Dear Lexis Advance,

I am applying for the position of legal research sales representative. I work as a legal editor and writer and I am a recent graduate of Name of University's School of Law and member of the Bar of the State of _____.

I am working this summer on a textbook analyzing domestic violence case law with a group of law school professors. I hope that it will one day assist attorneys representing victims of domestic violence. I am also editing several papers on various legal topics for a related law journal. As you will see from my resume, a major part of my writing and editing work involves legal research to check and support written work.

I hope that my scholarly work tells you that I am a dedicated and intelligent person who could be an asset in this position. I also hope that you will find my qualifications applicable and consider me for the position.

Sincerely,
Job Seeker
Job Seeker, Esq.

CHAPTER #5

FINDING POSTS AND APPLYING

Once you have your two or three resume versions and your cover letter formats created, then you are ready to apply to positions. You will also need to create a list of references. But because most positions ask for references at the interview, my discussion of how to create this additional document is addressed in the next chapter. For most positions, a cover letter and a resume are sufficient for the initial application. Your recently created LinkedIn profile will allow the employer to look a little more deeply into your qualifications after you apply and before they make a decision to interview you.

There will, however, be a few documents which will occasionally be requested at the application stage instead of later. The occasionally requested documents often include your list of references, unofficial school transcripts, and samples relevant to the industry (such as a "writing sample," which is an example of recent written work, such as a short course paper). Because you will need these at some point, you can either gather them now at this earlier stage in the job application process or later. Just use your judgment regarding if it makes sense to gather these now or wait until they are requested.

Your next step is to send your resume and cover letter out to potential employers. There are various ways to do this, including applying to posted positions (often called "job posts") and networking to find and apply for job openings. Strategies for making connections and networking, as well as some networking pitfalls, are addressed in a later chapter. This chapter addresses finding positions through job posts.

Job posts to which you should apply are any employment postings for positions for which you think you may be a good fit. My suggestion is that you identify several potentially good sources for these posts. Then apply to all posts that advertise positions that you would potentially want to have. Do not hesitate, just apply. Most applications will not result in interviews, so you will have to send out lots of resumes for a few interviews. Then, you can decline any position that you do not like well enough after the interview stage if it is offered. Getting resumes out in response to many posts is a good way to maximize interview (and therefore position) opportunities. Therefore, if you might like the job, send your resume.

Many people find positions by responding to posts. It can be a quick and successful way to identify an opening and directly match yourself to it. So, this is a key part of any job search. It is simply the submission of your qualifications, and showing your qualifications (skills and experiences, or just one experience) are a potential match to an open position.

Identify the locations of good posts for which you may be qualified in a few ways:

1. Regional trade or industry newspapers and publications can be an excellent source of local positions that meet your qualifications.

2. The career center at the school from which you graduated can be an excellent source of posts. This career center may also be able to help you to identify the applicable industry publications as well.

3. Libraries can provide significant access to industry periodicals and publications listing regional positions. They are also armed with lists of potentially fruitful regional listings and search engines.

4. You can develop a good list of websites to visit for individual companies or businesses in your area that regularly update employment postings. For example, a paralegal might create a list of the largest law firms in his area and regularly circle through those firm websites for new postings. He can create his list by searching for "large law firms in Washington D.C." (if he lives nearby).

5. You can visit various internet job posting boards regularly to find posts and apply for those positions.

6. Finally, you can team up with a recruiter (also called a "head hunter") whom you think may be able to find open positions for you. Just make sure that you are comfortable with the recruiter and how he works. For example, does he propose positions for your agreement, or does he send out your resume without advance permission from you? Are you precluded from applying to a

position if he has sent your resume to that company in the preceding several months or year? Finally, how is he compensated, and do you think that he will find posts which you cannot find, or otherwise promote you to companies well?

Once you identify any position through a post, I recommend that you apply. There is every reason to apply to a potentially good position immediately when you see it. If you also want to approach the business through a colleague, or in another manner (which is not too intrusive or pushy), then also do that. It is almost always more effective to apply and then seek out additional connections or follow up with a kind letter than to spend time networking or angling for the position at the outset when you have not yet applied.

I suggest that you apply right away with a solid resume and cover letter while the position remains open. Simply apply as soon as you see the post in the manner requested by the post and with the documents it requests. Often, this is as simple as emailing your resume and cover letter. The email can simply read "please accept my attached resume and cover letter as my application for the posted position entitled _____." Attach all documents that the post requests and no additional documents. For example, if it requests just a resume, then attach that and do not submit a cover letter. If it requests a resume, cover letter, and a list of references, then make sure to attach all three documents. If this post is worth it to you, then spend time finding connections and networking after you have applied. Do not delay in applying because the position may fill before you develop the connections or before a known connection gets around to forwarding your resume to the proper person.

Overall, the main idea is to develop a list of useful sources of job posts, apply liberally to posts, and do not delay your applications. Then, continue to revisit your sources for additional posts. Work on networking avenues for posts in which you are more interested after you have applied.

Another way to identify positions is through networking itself. Simply put, networking means making acquaintances in your field and developing those relationships into closer connections to increase your opportunities to find and obtain potential positions. It also includes working through longtime contacts and friends to find positions and increase the likelihood of getting them. People seeking to connect with employers by networking can go about it in varied ways. A later chapter discusses strategies for making connections and networking, as well as some common networking pitfalls.

CHAPTER #6

REFERENCES AND HELPING YOUR NEW EMPLOYER TO AVOID BAD INFLUENCES

Part One:

An Explanation of References and Where to Find Them

In addition to creating approximately three versions of your resume to more closely match your qualifications to job posts in which you are interested, and a cover letter (or a few such letters) that you will slightly tailor for each post, you will need to create a list of references.

This is a very short list, usually containing three work colleagues, professors, or teachers, who will speak highly of you to a potential employer. It is best if you can include a direct supervisor from a previous position on your list. Consider who to use as a reference carefully if you are applying to positions while employed at a job that you will later leave. Employers often consider seeking to leave their employ as a show of infidelity. They consistently and unfortunately react badly to your seeking employment elsewhere.

If you are transitioning to a new field, then you may be working in your old field still. If so, try to keep your search a secret from your current boss and do not use her (or anyone who will tell her) as a reference. You might even choose to insert a sentence into your cover letter saying "please keep my application for this position confidential, because I am not yet disclosing it to my current employer." It is better to use references from a different position, which you held for a company that you already left. That way, you have positive work references and little risk of backlash from your current employer.

Because you are job searching without experience, a good option is to request that current or former professors or teachers serve as your references. This is especially true if you are in your first position and keeping the search confidential, or if you are a current student or recent graduate. Simply ask them if they are comfortable with your including their name and work contact information on your list of references, which will result in potential employers calling them and their giving a positive reference for you. Then, provide each reference with your resume (or master resume list), so that each reference has something good to say about you nearby should they receive a call. You want your references to be prepared, even if you do not know them very well. You just want to make sure that they will provide a positive reference to any call or email from a potential employer. The information you provide will show them how you are qualified for the new field or position, and they can provide positive communications about you (a reference) in relation to it.

You will want to list about three references, their current position and company, in which capacity and where you worked together (or that they were your professor or teacher), and their current contact information (email and telephone being the most important, and U.S. postal address rarely being needed).

Part Two:

Example Lists of References

Here is an example list of references for a legal secretary who is transitioning to becoming an office manager of a law firm. Note, that she would only include people who are likely to be supportive. For example, she would not use her direct supervisor (and instead would use someone else) if she felt that her direct supervisor would undermine her.

Name
Address
Telephone Number
Email Address

Professional References

Person's name, Esq. (an associate with whom I worked closely at my prior firm)
Email address
Direct telephone number
Law firm name
City and state of law firm

Person's name, Esq. (the managing partner with whom I worked at my prior firm)
Email address
Direct telephone number
Law firm name
City and state of law firm

Person's name (the office manager, who was my direct supervisor at my prior firm)
Email address
Direct telephone number
Law firm name
City and state of law firm

Here is an example list of references for a recent graduate, who has not yet held a position. This recent graduate might choose to include information regarding her relationship with the professor, or not. Such as a parenthetical after the name stating "a professor from whom I learned how to use several industry relevant software formats."

Name
Address
Telephone Number
Email Address

Professional References

Professor's name, Ph.D., Name of University
Email address
Direct telephone number
City and state of University

Professor's name, Ph.D., Name of University
Email address
Direct telephone number
City and state of University

Professor's name, Ph.D., Name of University
Email address
Direct telephone number
City and state of University

CHAPTER #7

MINIMIZING "BAD INFLUENCES" AND DEALING WITH

HARMFUL PRIOR EMPLOYERS

People sometimes have difficulty finding new positions because of a "bad influence" from a prior workplace. Unfortunately, some people lose positions because of their prior boss. Happily, these might be people looking now to transition to a new career or field without experience in that field. They are upgrading without experience! This book, as well as this discussion of minimizing "bad influences," is for you.

A prior boss's bad decision that lost company business or had bad ramifications for the company, which was then couched by her to others as "this group was unproductive" or "this person was unproductive or inaccurate" can result in a lay off or job loss. You do not have knowledge of her dishonest communication to those still in the company, and they cannot easily confirm her lack of candor among themselves because she is their provider of information. Even if others suspect the issue was her fault, they often initially rally around her position if she is a major player who ousted a subordinate; it gives them a feeling of added security.

Therefore, you may want a strategy for minimizing this (or a similar) potential "bad influence" in your search for a much better future position. Here are a few such strategies:

First, you can structure your resume as strategized in this book by showcasing specific skills or highlighting specific examples of your work, rather than a chronological list of each employer and your functions in each position. These formats (specific skills and work examples as the resume structure) allow you to separate the "bad influence" from the skills gained in that position. The skills and/or experiences are showcased, not the position in which you gained them. Also, instead of a full list of positions held at the end of this resume, you can have a "list of major positions held," or "a list of most important positions held," or a "list of relevant positions held." This can further remove that old boss's harmful reach from impacting your well-deserved next position.

Second, you can direct all calls to the prior company to human resources, instead of your former boss. It is completely appropriate to tell a potential employer to call human resources and provide that number instead of the number of the "bad influence" herself. Most likely, you will not know if she is even still with the company.

Third, you can ask human resources what will be said to potential future employers who call for information. If it is just the dates worked, then you can rest more easily. This is often what human resources offices say if you were stellar and quit or stellar and let go by a "bad influence." You may also want to ask human resources to remind the "bad influence" of her obligation to provide no additional information and specifically no negative information about you to anyone.

Fourth, if you are let go, or leave, then you can ask a potential "bad influence" whether she would mind signing a simple letter of reference that you have attached to your email. If she does, or signs a version of it with which you are okay, then you can next send a thank you to her, which actually confirms with her that she will say nothing in addition to the letter about you to a potential future employer. You might write, "thank you for signing the letter of reference, I understand that this is what you will say to a future employer if called by them." Even if you do not provide the letter to any future employers (because it is likely very basic, and you can find better references), it is a way to understand the parameters of what she may say and to hold her accountable. She must proceed cautiously and conscientiously if she is called by a potential future employer because of your letter and her acquiescence to it (as shown by her signature). This works best for small business environments where human resources cannot shield you from the "bad influence" because there is no human resources department, and therefore, the "bad influence" is more likely to communicate directly with your potential future employers.

The problem with this technique is that a true "bad influence" is busy disingenuously promoting herself and may not choose to sign something contrary to her dishonest approach. She may act further hurtfully in response to your request. So, it may make sense to simply shield not only your future employer, but yourself from her "bad influence" and not interact with her at all.

Keep in mind, that being removed from that position is likely healthier for you than it felt to work with the "bad influence." Also, the company may have let her go after they let you go. A company sometimes lets the subordinate go and then the harmful boss. They receive the boss's information, rally around her for a time while she self-promotes, but later as the dust settles, her provision of information still does not make sense. It appears messy and out of place.

Some employers also let subordinates go first, so that the subordinate will not sue the company when the boss is let go. They worry that letting the boss go in front of the subordinate provides confirmation to the subordinate that they kept a "bad boss" for too long and that the "bad boss" hurt the subordinate's career. So the boss is let go at a later time, and it is couched as unrelated to the subordinate's job loss.

Just know that providing a clear, honest presentation of your skills and/or experiences will help you to move forward unencumbered.

CHAPTER #8

STRATEGIES FOR MAKING CONNECTIONS AND NETWORKING

You have identified your potential positions (by reviewing the posts to which you would consider applying). You have decided to apply to posts for a certain type of position, such as for the position of office manager, and you have created approximately two or three resumes, each demonstrating different strengths or experiences sought by businesses posting requests to fill that type of position. Your resumes highlight (for example) your personnel management skills in one version, your knowledge of small business health insurance plans or plan transitions in another version, and your skills budgeting and coordinating office purchases in the third version.

Then, you applied to various posts, and may have also sent resumes and cover letters to a few businesses that you have additionally identified as a potentially "good fit." Potentially, you have found these leads by a thorough update of LinkedIn and by seeking out connections on LinkedIn.

You may feel that you are starting to make real headway in your search and that you are hearing back from potential employers and/or LinkedIn connections. However, you may also feel that you are in a good preparatory position (having excellent resumes, an updated LinkedIn profile, and potential job postings), but that you have not yet connected with any potential employers.

People wanting to connect with employers through networking can go about it in varied ways. Let us discuss some potentially beneficial ways to network and some common pitfalls.

Part One:

A First Networking Strategy -

Developing a Quick Employee Acquaintance

and Then Sending a Letter to a Higher Up Decision-Maker

A potentially beneficial way to network with an employer is to meet someone who works for the business, learn something about this particular business, and then send a letter to a higher up decision-maker (who is not the person you have met, but who might make hiring decisions). The letter states that you have met an employee of the business (and names him) and that he has said several good things about the business (and tells what those things are). Then, your letter next states the type of position you are seeking and that you have noticed that this business has an opening, as listed on (named) site or post, or that you hope that the business might have an opening. You then enclose your resume and also send a connection request on LinkedIn. It is a good idea to send the letter and enclosure as attachments via email. Remember, you email the letter to the hiring decision-maker whom you have not met.

There are several reasons that this basic strategy can work: First, you want the likely decision-maker to see your resume.

Second, you have made the employer look good to the employer. The decision-maker has received a letter stating that his employee (or co-worker) is saying good things about the business and that his employee is making it look so good that he (the decision-maker) has been provided with a resume by a serious candidate for a position. The employer is likely to feel complimented. The employee (whom you met and with whom you briefly spoke) will look good to his employer because you have presented his positive statements about his job or the business to someone higher up in that business.

Third, if you have identified the incorrect decision-maker, your correspondence is fairly likely to be forwarded to the correct person because you are complimenting the business and its employee, and people like to look and feel good. Easy forwarding is the reason to send the letter and enclosure as attachments via email. This way, it can be circulated in the office as needed without any effort by the initial recipient. They will share it by email if it has arrived by email and can be forwarded with one click, but the recipient may not choose to share it if he has to scan it and create his own email.

Fourth, it is a fairly quick networking strategy because it can work with almost any employee that you are able to meet. It works quickly because you choose to whom to send your resume; it does not involve your having to meet the person to whom you wish to send the resume.

Fifth, you have made a basic connection that is not very deep (with the lower employee), and you have avoided a pitfall by not misrepresenting your connection. Misrepresenting the strength of a connection is a bad idea for a number of reasons. These include, not wanting to connect yourself in a significant way to someone whom you do not know. As well as not wanting to be "found out" to be pretending to be close to someone who says "I don't remember his name, but I might have met him at the recent seminar" because this undermines your veracity.

If there is an open position in that business that matches your resume, then this will hopefully create an interview for you. To increase that chance, make sure that your cover letter states any position posting that you have found online and that you are enclosing your resume as your application for that position. If there is no currently open position within this business, you will most likely receive a kind responsive email only.

Networking when a business does not have any openings is a big networking pitfall. Networking is best done in connection with a business that has current openings or that is large enough that openings arise on a regular basis. Therefore, gear these efforts to larger company environments that have openings or are likely to have openings regularly.

A networking pitfall is to spend too much time meeting people who are not likely to have an open position or likely future opening. Many people are not good at passing along the information from another person (the job seeker) to someone else whom they happen to know (another potential employer) that has or will have an opening of the right type. It is also unlikely that they know of someone with an opening. Because they are not searching for positions, they do not know of open positions in their colleagues' businesses. Mostly, they speak to one another about varied business issues that rarely involve discussions regarding how to find employees.

Also, when using any networking strategy (for any posted position or if a position is posted after you have begun to network with that company), then also send your resume and cover letter directly in response to the post. Send your resume and cover letter to human resources (or the specific person identified in the posting) in response to the post, even if you have already sent it to the decision-maker.

An additional networking pitfall is to rely on the decision-maker that you have identified to forward on your resume or to put in a good word for you along with forwarding your resume. He might just send a thank-you email to you, copy his secretary (without instruction to do anything with it), and leave it at that. Unfortunately, news of your application may not make it to human resources, despite the decision-maker in the group for which you might work, having your credentials and initial communication. By the time the interviews are scheduled, he has forgotten your letter, and human resources, having not been notified of your application, has not scheduled you for an interview with him and his group. Make sure the gatekeeper (here, human resources or the person listed in any job post) gets an application, not just the decision-maker for the applicable work group, because he does not schedule the interviews.

Overall, this initial networking approach involves applying for the position through posted channels, while making yourself known to the decision-maker for whom you might work. This is done in the hope that he might give you a boost because he has seen your credentials himself and liked them. You have made him feel positively in the letter, and you have made a slightly deeper connection with an employee through your meeting at a networking event or other avenue. It allows for a one-time meeting with someone who is not a leader in that business to grow into possible larger connections quickly.

Networking is time consuming, and meeting the exact right person is significantly difficult. So, a way to have that person (the decision-maker) read your letter is to positively discuss his current employee's positive statements about the company. You can simply ask the employee who you meet what he likes about where he works to elicit such a conversation. The decision-maker will want to read what is being said by his employee about the company (so he will finish reading the letter you send). By keeping your letter entirely positive, you make him feel good about his business and you make your employee acquaintance look good too. This can "grow" your relationship with the employee. You can also show how you would be a "good fit" in that work group through this style of networking (you appear amenable and to get along with employees).

To "grow" your connection with the employee and/or the decision-maker, you may want to forward the employee an email with a copy of the letter that you sent to the decision-maker. It is up to you whether to openly carbon copy (cc) the employee on the email to the decision-maker. Strategically, if you have said positive things about the employee to the decision-maker, and the decision-maker does not think the employee knows, then he may tell the employee that he is being positively discussed by someone he met at an event or recent seminar. This means that they might have a conversation about you. If you think that this conversation will benefit you, then it might be strategic to not inform the decision-maker that you sent the correspondence to the employee you met. To do this, just blind carbon copy (bcc) the employee on the initial email to the decision-maker.

The strategy works because the employee remembers you when he reads your letter (sent as a blind carbon copy or even an entirely separate email). From reading the letter, he knows you complimented him, and he is prepared if the decision-maker drops into his office to say it is nice to hear about the good things he is saying to others about the business. If your impression on the employee was favorable, then the employee might say something good about you to the decision-maker too. He might like the idea of you filling the position because you made him look good to a company higher up or co-worker, after only a simple, initial meeting. You have encouraged a conversation about yourself where you might be complimented to the decision-maker by his own employee through a single meeting with any employee, and a letter to the decision-maker with a blind carbon copy to the employee. They are more likely to talk to one another if the decision-maker does not know that you already informed the employee that you transmitted his positive comments to his employer, and you have prepared the employee to speak kindly of you by sending him the complimentary correspondence too.

Part Two:

A Second Networking Strategy -

Carefully Considering When to Apply Through a Good Friend

A second networking issue involves considering when to apply to a business through a good friend (who works there) and when not to. I recommend contextualizing your friend as a business acquaintance and downplaying your closeness when applying.

If you have a friend who is not a hiring decision-maker, then it is tempting to request that your friend bring your resume to that decision-maker and vouch for your "good fit" and "known responsibility" in a conversation with the decision-maker. Your friend simply does you a favor by bringing in your resume and requesting that you be interviewed for a current or potential opening. This is in fact a networking situation that many people spend a great deal of time angling to create. They try to increase relationships to enable them to have this very presentation of their resume by a real friend. The closer the connection the better, they think.

There are however, many problems with this as a networking strategy. The first problem is that employers often do not want employees to be close out-of-office friends who met one another prior to working together. There are several potential problems with close friendships from an employer's perspective. One is the potential for mutual distraction when friends work together. Another is the boss's feeling that she might eventually be outnumbered or undermined because the friend employees will discuss the boss's office decisions and agree (or partially agree) that their boss (or co-worker who is the hiring decision-maker) should not have made a decision (or proceeded in this way on a project) which they decide has negatively affected the business or work group. The boss or co-worker (who is the hiring decision-maker) does not want to feel that the hiring decision will bring in a new team member who is too closely connected to another team member because it counterbalances her presence in the office as a weightier player or equal part.

Another problem with this as a networking strategy is the employer or deciding co-worker may not like the employee as much as your friend thinks that she is liked. Even though she is a good, steady, and a rising employee, you run the risk of attaching your credentials to her prior and current negative office relationships. Any employee rising through the ranks, is liked by some, and often still perceived by some others in a negative way. Your attachment to her positive office standing also attaches you to the negative perceptions of her as well.

This coupled with the idea that two friends will bond together and potentially off-balance other team members means that her provision of your resume may not help you or her. Some networking strategists would argue that your (hopefully savvy) friend will know her position in the business and that you, as her friend, can trust her to position you too. This presumes (over simplistically) that if the employer likes her, they will be more inclined to interview you than a candidate from a cold resume drop.

I think that there is a better way to connect to the office through a friend that can avoid the friendship networking pitfall. Your friend can couch your relationship with her as one that is primarily or entirely professional, and she can speak highly of you. She still separates your resume from the masses, without offsetting her boss's or coworker's perception of you or her in any way.

You may consider asking her to contextualize your relationship as less close by saying something like "we went to law school together (or college, or worked together previously, so long as one of these are true), and she and I recently re-connected through mutual acquaintances (or at an event) and she mentioned that she is looking to transition. I remember her as being very hard working (in school or in the prior position, whichever is true), and her credentials look good to me. So, I'm sending her resume along to you. I'm probably going to take her to lunch sometime soon, would you like to come?"

If asked, your friend, whom you are contextualizing as a business acquaintance for job-seeking purposes, can say that she obtained your resume from LinkedIn (provided that it is attached to LinkedIn), that you sent it to her, or that she requested it from you. You are downplaying your friendship and increasing the perceived space between you two in this conversation. This is sound networking strategy, even though it is contrary to many networking enthusiasts advice to flaunt close connections.

Decreasing the perception of your friendship helps to professionalize your relationship and helps you to avoid the pitfalls of having a close friend provide your resume to her employer. It also avoids your looking like she is doing a favor for you. The employer or decision-maker would prefer that she did a favor for them. If she brings in a resume of an acquaintance who she thinks would be good for the position, she is perceived to be doing a favor for the employer; she is looking out for someone good, or came across someone good by happenstance. If she brings in a friend's resume, she is perceived to be doing a favor for the friend (not the employer).

Remember that your context for the relationship needs to be true (to say that you know each other from law school, you must have gone to law school together). Downplaying your relationship, is however, not dishonest. Even if you are good friends, you can contextualize your relationship as not as close and increase your professional connection.

If found out later to be good friends, you simply mention that you did not want to request favoritism or make the employer uncomfortable. She might have been uncomfortable if she were perceived to have denied a current solid employee's qualified good friend the position. Since most people who apply to any job are not hired, the current employee did not want to make the employer feel uncomfortable if she did not like the candidate/friend for the position.

This smooths the way for your friend to recommend you (or for you to recommend yourself) for a different company position if you are not hired or do not get this position. Also, if you do get the job, you and your friend can continue to contextualize your relationship professionally, so that you are not perceived as counterbalancing team players in any unprofessional manner. If you are not going to distract one another or otherwise act unprofessionally, then it is completely acceptable to contextualize your relationship as professional acquaintances because that is how you will relate to one another during office hours.

CHAPTER #9

INTERVIEWING AND WHEN TO DISCUSS MONEY

Part One:

The Interview Overview

For an interview, dress well, arrive early, and bring with you all of the documents that you previously sent to the company as well the remaining documents that they might need to make a decision (even if you were not asked for them yet). The documents are most likely to include:

- Your resume;
- Your list of references;
- Your transcript (if you think that they may need it to offer you the position); and
- Any sample of your work that is usual in your field (such as a writing sample).

If the interview goes well, and you outshine the competition, then you have all of the documents that the company will eventually need in order to offer you the position. Simply have them with you, and you can provide them on the spot, if asked (rather than by email later). Then, when you leave the interview, they already have everything they need to make a quicker offer. You are not at home the next day scrambling to find references, while they are trying to make quick hiring decisions.

To outshine the competition on the interview, you will need to prepare. You will want to prepare in three ways:

First, re-read the post, especially the requested qualifications for the applicant. Also, review the company's website and learn about it. You do not need to know everything; just a basic understanding of the company and a more thorough review of the post will suffice. The interview is not about your knowledge of the company, it is about how your qualifications fit the spot they need to fill.

Second, thoroughly review your master resume list (the list you created and from which you developed two or three resumes). Renew your understanding of your skills and experiences and how they can fit the position's needs. Also, review the version of the resume that you used to apply for the position.

Third, practice discussing how your skills and experiences fit the qualifications being sought for the position. Do this by talking to another person or by just pretending you are at the interview. Practicing this will prepare you to answer questions about your qualifications for the position. You will be specifically prepared to explain how your background fits their needs. Fitting you to the position is the main item on an interviewer's agenda. Part two of this chapter discusses this in greater detail.

Even if you are not entirely certain that this is the position for you while interviewing, pretend that you are certain you will love it. You can make a decision about taking the job after you have an offer, but you cannot get an offer if you do not appear to be certain that the position is a good fit.

Discuss money only if you are directly asked about your salary requirements. Otherwise, wait until you receive an offer. Discussing money during an interview, when you do not yet have the position, appears presumptuous (that you will receive an offer) and distasteful. You want an entirely positive interview, without any negativity.

Also, if you propose a number that is too low, you cheat yourself out of a potentially higher offer by jumping ahead. Once the position is offered, you can try to negotiate a low offer up, or be happy that the offer is a good one. At the offer stage they know they want you for the position, so you are in a stronger position then you were in at the interview. Only bring up your salary requirement at the interview stage if it is truly a requirement, meaning that you know that you do not want the offer unless it is a certain salary amount. But because you are not significantly familiar with this new field or salary range for this type of position, and you are just now learning about the work hours, the job details, and the work environment, it is likely too early to set the number at the interview. You want them to want you, and you want to gather information to see if you want them too.

Know that you are potentially diminishing your chances for an offer by providing a number when it was not yet requested. It is worth it to wait for the offer and negotiate then. You will also have had some time to consider what you think of the company, the position, the responsibility, the hours, and how you feel about working there. You can consider what the job is worth to you while you wait to see if it is offered.

Part Two:

How to Discuss Skills, Single Experiences, and Coursework

For What They Are - Qualifications for the Position

Recall from earlier in the book that it is important to be an enthusiastic proponent of your experience. If you meet with skepticism, such as a truculent interviewer's statement of "I am not sure that coursework, skill gained outside of employment, or a single experience is applicable work experience. I am used to reading about actual work experience on a resume." Then, politely and happily state that you are very much looking forward to new experiences in a company environment and that you have a significant amount of current knowledge (for example from coursework or a very recent single experience) to offer.

I recommend that you do not directly argue in an interview setting about the validity of applying coursework and skills based on single experience examples in the place of the interviewers regularly seen qualifications. Instead, positively and charismatically reiterate your excitement to work for this company, and state that you have a significant amount of knowledge gained from the coursework and single experiences, or reiterate why you are skilled in this area. Communicate that you are seeking this opportunity because you will be good at it. Further, that you know that you will be good at it because you have the understanding and knowledge that the position needs as demonstrated by your coursework, excellent grades, and resulting degree. Or that you know you will be good at it because of the excellent results you achieved in your single experience. Explain why you know you can do this job well.

Remember, you are overcoming the tricky issue of needing experience to get the job and the job to get experience. Never let an interview turn into an argument of whether coursework or example-based experience is exactly right. Almost no prior experience is exactly right for every position. Just discuss the qualities that make you a good fit (even if you have to dodge the question a bit). Respond to a question that implies your coursework, skills or single experiences are insufficient by stating that you: have current knowledge in the field (shown by your degree and major, or relevant single experience); are a high-level thinker (shown by your grade point average, school attended, and completion of a bachelor's degree, or by explaining your skill based knowledge); dress appropriately; arrive promptly; are great to work with; and put the needed time and effort into each project. These qualities are certainly applicable to the position. Plus, your resume was selected for an interview, showing that your coursework, skills, or single experiences have already been well received by some in the company.

Remember that experience is built from the ground up, so we simply characterize what we have (be it coursework, a single experience, or a skill) to convince someone that we are ready for the position we want. Then we use that to build experience for the next position, and again re-characterize our experience to take the leap for which we are ready (but despite our readiness, for which we do not yet have any depth of experience; we only have limited experience).

You are ready for that next position, so showcase yourself by showcasing what you can do next, rather than what you have done already!

CHAPTER #10

THE WORKBOOK

Identify Your Next Position

Identify the "type of position" that you are seeking. Set a goal to get it and list your qualifications for it. Start by making a list of the positions you might want to have as your next position:

_____

_____

_____

_____

_____

_____

_____

_____

_____

_____

_____

_____

Then, narrow down your list. Of these positions the one that you will pursue is:

_____

_____

_____

_____

_____

List the Qualifications Employers Want for the Position You Seek

Make a list of the main qualifications employers want for the position you are seeking. Find these qualifications in job posts written by prospective employers. The posts will say which qualifications the employer is looking for in an employee for a certain position.

-
-
-
-
-
-
-
-
-
-
-
-
-

List Your Qualifications for the Position

Now, draft a list of those things which the employer needs, which you know you can do. These are your qualifications for the position.

-
-
-
-
-
-
-
-
-
-
-
-
-
-
-
-
-
-
-
-

Create a Draft Master Resume List

Write a paragraph for each of your qualifications for the position. These paragraphs describe and explain your qualifications. Describe each qualification and explain why you know you can do it. Skip ahead to read about using single experiences, work done in part-time unrelated positions, and coursework examples, if you plan to use those primarily. Then, draft this master list afterwards. Or, progress through the workbook in the order written and add detail later as you get better at explaining each type of qualification which is relevant to you. There is a space later for a final master resume list which will showcase all of the descriptions that you will create in this workbook.

You are qualified to:

_____

_____

_____

_____

Describe what you can do:

_____

_____

_____

_____

_____

_____

_____

_____

Explain why you know you can do it:

_____

_____

_____

_____

_____

_____

_____

_____

_____

_____

_____

_____

_____

_____

_____

_____

_____

_____

You are qualified to:

_____

_____

_____

_____

Describe what you can do:

_____

_____

_____

_____

_____

_____

_____

_____

Explain why you know you can do it:

_____

_____

_____

_____

_____

_____

_____

_____

_____

_____

_____

_____

_____

You are qualified to:

_____

_____

_____

Describe what you can do:

_____

_____

_____

_____

_____

_____

_____

_____

Explain why you know you can do it:

_____

_____

_____

_____

_____

_____

_____

_____

_____

_____

_____

_____

You are qualified to:

_____

_____

_____

_____

Describe what you can do:

_____

_____

_____

_____

_____

_____

_____

Explain why you know you can do it:

_____

_____

_____

_____

_____

_____

_____

_____

_____

_____

_____

_____

You are qualified to:

_____

_____

_____

_____

Describe what you can do:

_____

_____

_____

_____

_____

_____

_____

_____

Explain why you know you can do it:

_____

_____

_____

_____

_____

_____

_____

_____

_____

_____

_____

_____

You are qualified to:

_____

_____

_____

_____

Describe what you can do:

_____

_____

_____

_____

_____

_____

_____

Explain why you know you can do it:

_____

_____

_____

_____

_____

_____

_____

_____

_____

_____

_____

You are qualified to:

_____

_____

_____

Describe what you can do:

_____

_____

_____

_____

_____

_____

_____

_____

Explain why you know you can do it:

_____

_____

_____

_____

_____

_____

_____

_____

_____

_____

_____

_____

You are qualified to:

_____

_____

_____

_____

Describe what you can do:

_____

_____

_____

_____

_____

_____

_____

_____

Explain why you know you can do it:

_____

_____

_____

_____

_____

_____

_____

_____

_____

_____

_____

_____

You are qualified to:

_____

_____

_____

_____

Describe what you can do:

_____

_____

_____

_____

_____

_____

_____

_____

Explain why you know you can do it:

_____

_____

_____

_____

_____

_____

_____

_____

_____

_____

_____

_____

Add the Remaining Components to Your Master List

Educational Background

Add the remaining components to the master list. Describe your educational background.

List relevant schools, graduation dates, training, and significant testing: _____

_____

_____

_____

_____

_____

_____

_____

_____

Prior Positions

Next, delineate any work history. Make a list of any prior positions, the names of the businesses you worked for, and the dates you worked for them.

List of prior positions, businesses, and dates of employment: _____

_____

_____

_____

_____

_____

_____

_____

_____

_____

Arrange Three Draft Resumes from Your Draft Master Resume List

Arrange three resumes for this position from your master list. Remember, consider skipping ahead to practice describing single experiences, unrelated part-time positions, and coursework if you plan to use them and do not plan to revise your descriptions later. There is a space later for a three final resumes which will showcase all of the descriptions that you will create in this workbook.

The First Resume

The position you seek:

_____

_____

The main types of qualifications you will highlight in this resume version are:

_____

_____

_____

_____

_____

The paragraphs which you will include from your master resume list include the following.

First:

_____

_____

_____

_____

_____

_____

_____

_____

_____

_____

Second:

_____

_____

_____

_____

_____

_____

_____

_____

_____

_____

Third:

_____

_____

_____

_____

_____

_____

_____

_____

_____

Fourth:

_____

_____

_____

_____

_____

_____

_____

_____

_____

_____

_____

_____

_____

Fifth:

_____

_____

_____

_____

_____

_____

_____

_____

_____

_____

Education to include:

_____

_____

_____

_____

_____

_____

_____

_____

Any prior positions to include:

_____

_____

_____

_____

_____

_____

_____

_____

The Second Resume

The position you seek:

_____

_____

The main types of qualifications you will highlight in this resume version are:

_____

_____

_____

_____

_____

The paragraphs which you will include from your master resume list include the following.

First:

_____

_____

_____

_____

_____

_____

_____

_____

_____

_____

_____

Second:

_____

_____

_____

_____

_____

_____

_____

_____

_____

_____

Third:

_____

_____

_____

_____

_____

_____

_____

_____

_____

_____

Fourth:

_____

_____

_____

_____

_____

_____

_____

_____

_____

Fifth:

_____

_____

_____

_____

_____

_____

_____

_____

_____

Education to include:

_____

_____

_____

_____

_____

_____

_____

_____

_____

_____

Any prior positions to include:

_____

_____

_____

_____

_____

_____

_____

_____

The Third Resume

The position you seek:

_____

_____

The main types of qualifications you will highlight in this resume version are:

_____

_____

_____

_____

_____

The paragraphs which you will include from your master resume list include the following.

First:

_____

_____

_____

_____

_____

_____

_____

_____

_____

_____

_____

Second:

_____

_____

_____

_____

_____

_____

_____

_____

_____

_____

Third:

_____

_____

_____

_____

_____

_____

_____

_____

_____

_____

Fourth:

_____

_____

_____

_____

_____

_____

_____

_____

_____

_____

_____

Fifth:

_____

_____

_____

_____

_____

_____

_____

_____

_____

Education to include:

_____

_____

_____

_____

_____

_____

_____

_____

_____

Any prior positions to include:

_____

_____

_____

_____

_____

_____

_____

_____

Describe Single Experiences

Describe single experiences to show that you are good at doing something which you have only done once. Add these paragraphs to your master resume list and resumes if they help to substantiate your qualifications. Improve upon your work as you find better ways to describe and explain your qualifications.

Describe a single experience:

_____

_____

_____

_____

_____

_____

_____

_____

_____

Now, explain how it shows that you can do a necessary task for the job you seek:

_____

_____

_____

_____

_____

_____

_____

_____

_____

_____

Describe another single experience:

_____

_____

_____

_____

_____

_____

_____

_____

_____

Now, explain how it shows that you can do a necessary task for the job you seek:

_____

_____

_____

_____

_____

_____

_____

_____

_____

Describe another single experience:

_____

_____

_____

_____

_____

_____

_____

_____

Now, explain how it shows that you can do a necessary task for the job you seek:

_____

_____

_____

_____

_____

_____

_____

_____

Describe another single experience:

_____

_____

_____

_____

_____

_____

Now, explain how it shows that you can do a necessary task for the job you seek:

_____

_____

_____

_____

_____

_____

_____

_____

Describe another single experience:

_____

_____

_____

_____

_____

_____

_____

_____

_____

Now, explain how it shows that you can do a necessary task for the job you seek:

_____

_____

_____

_____

_____

_____

_____

_____

Describe Skills from Unrelated Part-Time Work

Describe a skill that is needed in the position you seek which you gained from a dissimilar part-time job.

The skill needed by the employer is:

_____

_____

_____

Describe what you can do based on your part-time experience:

_____

_____

_____

_____

_____

_____

_____

_____

_____

_____

_____

Explain that you are qualified to perform the skill needed by the employer:

_____

_____

_____

_____

_____

_____

_____

_____

_____

_____

Another skill needed by the employer is:

_____

_____

_____

_____

_____

Describe what you can do based on your part-time experience:

_____

_____

_____

_____

_____

_____

_____

_____

_____

_____

_____

Explain that you are qualified to perform the skill needed by the employer:

_____

_____

_____

_____

_____

_____

_____

_____

_____

_____

_____

_____

Another skill needed by the employer is:

_____

_____

_____

Describe what you can do based on your part-time experience:

_____

_____

_____

_____

_____

_____

Explain that you are qualified to perform the skill needed by the employer:

Another skill needed by the employer is:

_____

_____

_____

Describe what you can do based on your part-time experience:

_____

_____

_____

_____

_____

_____

_____

_____

_____

_____

_____

Explain that you are qualified to perform the skill needed by the employer:

_____

_____

_____

_____

_____

_____

_____

_____

_____

_____

_____

Another skill needed by the employer is:

_____

_____

Describe what you can do based on your part-time experience:

_____

_____

_____

_____

_____

_____

_____

_____

_____

_____

_____

Explain that you are qualified to perform the skill needed by the employer:

_____

_____

_____

_____

_____

_____

_____

_____

Create Specific Examples of Your Qualifications from Coursework

Create specific examples of your qualifications directly from coursework or studies by explaining the knowledge and skills you have gained in college.

Explain relevant knowledge gained from coursework:

_____

_____

_____

_____

_____

_____

_____

_____

List tests of the topic and successful grades:

_____

_____

_____

_____

_____

_____

_____

_____

_____

Explain course projects where you demonstrated your knowledge:

_____

_____

_____

_____

_____

_____

_____

_____

Describe other ways in which you have demonstrated knowledge, gained in coursework, which is needed by the employer:

I know how to:

_____

_____

_____

_____

_____

_____

I gained this knowledge from the following coursework:

_____

_____

_____

_____

_____

I have demonstrated my knowledge by doing the following:

_____

_____

_____

_____

_____

_____

_____

_____

_____

_____

Your job posting states that you need this type of skill, and I can use this skill in your office by:

_____

_____

_____

_____

_____

_____

_____

_____

Explain relevant knowledge gained from coursework:

_____

_____

_____

_____

_____

_____

_____

_____

List tests of the topic and successful grades:

_____

_____

_____

_____

_____

_____

_____

_____

Explain course projects where you demonstrated your knowledge:

_____

_____

_____

_____

_____

_____

_____

_____

_____

Describe other ways in which you have demonstrated knowledge, gained in coursework, which is needed by the employer:

I know how to:

_____

_____

_____

_____

_____

_____

_____

I gained this knowledge from the following coursework:

_____

_____

_____

_____

_____

_____

_____

I have demonstrated my knowledge by doing the following:

_____

_____

_____

_____

_____

_____

_____

_____

_____

_____

_____

_____

Your job posting states that you need this type of skill, and I can use this skill in your office by:

_____

_____

_____

_____

_____

_____

_____

_____

_____

_____

Explain relevant knowledge gained from coursework:

_____

_____

_____

_____

_____

_____

_____

_____

List tests of the topic and successful grades:

_____

_____

_____

_____

_____

_____

_____

_____

Explain course projects where you demonstrated your knowledge:

_____

_____

_____

_____

_____

_____

_____

_____

Describe other ways in which you have demonstrated knowledge, gained in coursework, which is needed by the employer:

I know how to:

_____

_____

_____

_____

_____

_____

I gained this knowledge from the following coursework:

_____

_____

_____

_____

_____

_____

_____

I have demonstrated my knowledge by doing the following:

_____

_____

_____

_____

_____

_____

_____

_____

_____

_____

_____

Your job posting states that you need this type of skill, and I can use this skill in your office by:

_____

_____

_____

_____

_____

_____

_____

_____

Explain relevant knowledge gained from coursework:

_____

_____

_____

_____

_____

_____

_____

_____

List tests of the topic and successful grades:

_____

_____

_____

_____

_____

_____

_____

_____

Explain course projects where you demonstrated your knowledge:

_____

_____

_____

_____

_____

_____

_____

_____

Describe other ways in which you have demonstrated knowledge, gained in coursework, which is needed by the employer:

I know how to:

_____

_____

_____

_____

_____

_____

_____

I gained this knowledge from the following coursework:

_____

_____

_____

_____

_____

_____

_____

I have demonstrated my knowledge by doing the following:

_____

_____

_____

_____

_____

_____

_____

_____

_____

_____

_____

_____

Your job posting states that you need this type of skill, and I can use this skill in your office by:

_____

_____

_____

_____

_____

_____

_____

_____

_____

Explain relevant knowledge gained from coursework:

_____

_____

_____

_____

_____

_____

_____

_____

List tests of the topic and successful grades:

_____

_____

_____

_____

_____

_____

_____

_____

Explain course projects where you demonstrated your knowledge:

_____

_____

_____

_____

_____

_____

_____

_____

Describe other ways in which you have demonstrated knowledge, gained in coursework, which is needed by the employer:

I know how to:

_____

_____

_____

_____

_____

_____

I gained this knowledge from the following coursework:

_____

_____

_____

_____

_____

_____

I have demonstrated my knowledge by doing the following:

_____

_____

_____

_____

_____

_____

_____

_____

_____

_____

_____

Your job posting states that you need this type of skill, and I can use this skill in your office by:

_____

_____

_____

_____

_____

_____

_____

_____

_____

_____

Explain relevant knowledge gained from coursework:

_____

_____

_____

_____

_____

_____

_____

_____

List tests of the topic and successful grades:

_____

_____

_____

_____

_____

_____

_____

_____

Explain course projects where you demonstrated your knowledge:

_____

_____

_____

_____

_____

_____

_____

_____

Describe other ways in which you have demonstrated knowledge, gained in coursework, which is needed by the employer:

I know how to:

_____

_____

_____

_____

_____

_____

I gained this knowledge from the following coursework:

_____

_____

_____

_____

_____

_____

_____

I have demonstrated my knowledge by doing the following:

_____

_____

_____

_____

_____

_____

_____

_____

_____

_____

_____

Your job posting states that you need this type of skill, and I can use this skill in your office by:

_____

_____

_____

_____

_____

_____

_____

_____

_____

Prepare For the Interview As You Draft Your Resume

Prepare for the interview as you go along. Consider how to discuss these examples as qualifications. Do this by explaining what you know you are qualified to do and how the coursework prepared you. Practice making these statements:

I can: _____

_____

_____

_____

_____

_____

_____

_____

_____

_____

I gained this skill (or learned this skill) when: _____

_____

_____

_____

_____

_____

_____

_____

_____

_____

_____

I demonstrated my skills, which qualify me to work for you, by passing these tests:

_____

_____

_____

_____

_____

_____

_____

_____

_____

_____

I am ready to apply this skill in a company environment because: _____

_____

_____

_____

_____

_____

_____

_____

_____

_____

_____

I can: _____

_____

_____

_____

_____

_____

_____

_____

_____

I gained this skill (or learned this skill) when: _____

_____

_____

_____

_____

_____

_____

_____

_____

_____

I demonstrated my skills, which qualify me to work for you, by passing these tests:

_____

_____

_____

_____

_____

_____

_____

_____

_____

I am ready to apply this skill in a company environment because: _____

_____

_____

_____

_____

_____

_____

_____

_____

_____

_____

I can: _____

_____

_____

_____

_____

_____

_____

_____

_____

_____

I gained this skill (or learned this skill) when: _____

_____

_____

_____

_____

_____

_____

_____

_____

_____

_____

I demonstrated my skills, which qualify me to work for you, by passing these tests:

_____

_____

_____

_____

_____

_____

_____

_____

I am ready to apply this skill in a company environment because: _____

_____

_____

_____

_____

_____

_____

_____

_____

_____

_____

_____

I can: _____

_____

_____

_____

_____

_____

_____

_____

_____

I gained this skill (or learned this skill) when: _____

_____

_____

_____

_____

_____

_____

_____

_____

_____

_____

I demonstrated my skills, which qualify me to work for you, by passing these tests:

_____

_____

_____

_____

_____

_____

_____

_____

_____

I am ready to apply this skill in a company environment because: _____

_____

_____

_____

_____

_____

_____

_____

_____

_____

_____

I can: _____

_____

_____

_____

_____

_____

_____

_____

_____

_____

I gained this skill (or learned this skill) when: _____

_____

_____

_____

_____

_____

_____

_____

_____

_____

_____

I demonstrated my skills, which qualify me to work for you, by passing these tests:

_____

_____

_____

_____

_____

_____

_____

_____

_____

_____

I am ready to apply this skill in a company environment because: _____

_____

_____

_____

_____

_____

_____

_____

_____

_____

_____

Practice Promoting Your Qualifications

When it is suggested that coursework is not relevant experience, be ready to positively communicate that you have the skills needed to perform the job well. Fill in the table with example statements from Chapter #2, Part Three: Explaining that Coursework is Experience to a Potential Employer, and add your own statements as well.

An interviewer might argue that coursework is not relevant experience. He might say:	My response will be that I have the skills needed to perform the job well. I will say:

Make a Career Plan

Make a plan for progressive career improvement. Consider what you would like to do in the long run, then plan the steps to get there. Plan to stretch to obtain a position to gain experience, then stretch to obtain a better position to climb the ladder you envision.

List a position that you would ultimately like to have: _____

_____

_____

_____

_____

_____

Then chart the possible steps to get there.

Step one. The position is: _____

_____

_____

_____

The skills you will gain in this position are: _____

_____

_____

_____

_____

An idea for step two. The position is: _____

_____

_____

_____

The skills you will gain in this position are: _____

_____

_____

_____

An idea for step three. The position is: _____

_____

_____

_____

The skills you will gain in this position are: _____

_____

_____

_____

_____

_____

An idea for step four. The position is: _____

_____

_____

_____

The skills you will gain in this position are: _____

_____

_____

_____

List how these skills will all add up to qualify you for the ultimate position which you would like to have: _____

_____

_____

_____

_____

_____

_____

_____

_____

Final Master Resume List

Write a final paragraph for each of your qualifications for the position. Make sure to fully describe each qualification and explain why you know you can do it. Use all of your qualifications, including single experiences, work done in part-time unrelated positions, and coursework examples to explain each type of qualification which is relevant to you. Then type this master list. You can electronically cut and paste these paragraphs into three final resume versions. Or, you can handwrite the final three resume versions in this workbook before typing them.

You are qualified to:

_____

_____

_____

_____

Describe what you can do:

_____

_____

_____

_____

_____

_____

_____

_____

Explain why you know you can do it:

_____

_____

_____

_____

_____

_____

_____

_____

_____

_____

_____

_____

_____

_____

_____

_____

_____

You are qualified to:

_____

_____

_____

_____

Describe what you can do:

_____

_____

_____

_____

_____

_____

_____

Explain why you know you can do it:

_____

_____

_____

_____

_____

_____

_____

_____

_____

_____

_____

You are qualified to:

_____

_____

_____

_____

Describe what you can do:

_____

_____

_____

_____

_____

_____

_____

_____

_____

Explain why you know you can do it:

_____

_____

_____

_____

_____

_____

_____

_____

_____

_____

_____

_____

You are qualified to:

_____

_____

_____

_____

Describe what you can do:

_____

_____

_____

_____

_____

_____

_____

Explain why you know you can do it:

_____

_____

_____

_____

_____

_____

_____

_____

_____

_____

_____

You are qualified to:

_____

_____

_____

Describe what you can do:

_____

_____

_____

_____

_____

Explain why you know you can do it:

You are qualified to:

_____

_____

_____

_____

Describe what you can do:

_____

_____

_____

_____

_____

_____

_____

Explain why you know you can do it:

_____

_____

_____

_____

_____

_____

_____

_____

_____

_____

_____

You are qualified to:

_____

_____

_____

_____

Describe what you can do:

_____

_____

_____

_____

_____

_____

_____

_____

Explain why you know you can do it:

_____

_____

_____

_____

_____

_____

_____

_____

_____

_____

_____

_____

You are qualified to:

_____

_____

_____

_____

Describe what you can do:

_____

_____

_____

_____

_____

_____

_____

_____

Explain why you know you can do it:

_____

_____

_____

_____

_____

_____

_____

_____

_____

_____

_____

_____

You are qualified to:

_____

_____

_____

_____

Describe what you can do:

_____

_____

_____

_____

_____

_____

_____

_____

Explain why you know you can do it:

_____

_____

_____

_____

_____

_____

_____

_____

_____

_____

_____

_____

Educational Background

Add the remaining components to the master list. Describe your educational background.

List relevant schools, graduation dates, training, and significant testing: _____

_____

_____

_____

_____

_____

_____

_____

_____

Prior Positions

Next, delineate any work history. Make a list of any prior positions, the names of the businesses you worked for, and the dates you worked for them.

List of prior positions, businesses, and dates of employment: _____

_____

_____

_____

_____

_____

_____

_____

_____

_____

Your Final Three Resumes For Typing

Arrange your three final resumes for this position from your master list. Describe single experiences, unrelated part-time positions, and coursework as you plan to use them. Then, type your three resume versions and proofread them.

The First Resume

The position you seek:

_____

_____

The main types of qualifications you will highlight in this resume version are:

_____

_____

_____

_____

_____

The paragraphs which you will include from your master resume list include the following.

First:

_____

_____

_____

_____

_____

_____

_____

_____

_____

_____

_____

Second:

_____

_____

_____

_____

_____

_____

_____

_____

_____

_____

Third:

_____

_____

_____

_____

_____

_____

_____

_____

_____

_____

Fourth:

_____

_____

_____

_____

_____

_____

_____

_____

_____

_____

_____

_____

Fifth:

_____

_____

_____

_____

_____

_____

_____

_____

_____

_____

Education to include:

_____

_____

_____

_____

_____

_____

_____

Any prior positions to include:

_____

_____

_____

_____

_____

_____

The Second Resume

The position you seek:

_____

_____

The main types of qualifications you will highlight in this resume version are:

_____

_____

_____

_____

_____

The paragraphs which you will include from your master resume list include the following.

First:

_____

_____

_____

_____

_____

_____

_____

_____

_____

_____

_____

Second:

_____

_____

_____

_____

_____

_____

_____

_____

_____

Third:

_____

_____

_____

_____

_____

_____

_____

_____

_____

_____

Fourth:

_____

_____

_____

_____

_____

_____

_____

_____

_____

_____

Fifth:

_____

_____

_____

_____

_____

_____

_____

_____

_____

Education to include:

_____

_____

_____

_____

_____

_____

_____

_____

_____

_____

Any prior positions to include:

_____

_____

_____

_____

_____

_____

_____

_____

The Third Resume

The position you seek:

_____

_____

The main types of qualifications you will highlight in this resume version are:

_____

_____

_____

_____

_____

The paragraphs which you will include from your master resume list include the following.

First:

_____

_____

_____

_____

_____

_____

_____

_____

_____

_____

_____

Second:

_____

_____

_____

_____

_____

_____

_____

_____

_____

_____

Third:

_____

_____

_____

_____

_____

_____

_____

_____

_____

_____

Fourth:

_____

_____

_____

_____

_____

_____

_____

_____

_____

_____

Fifth:

_____

_____

_____

_____

_____

_____

_____

_____

Education to include:

_____

_____

_____

_____

_____

_____

_____

_____

_____

_____

Any prior positions to include:

_____

_____

_____

_____

_____

_____

_____

_____

_____

List Those with Whom You Will Connect On LinkedIn

Write a list of those people with whom you plan to connect on LinkedIn.

Name and business:	Contact information:

List Those to Whom You Will Email Your Resume

Write an additional list of those people to whom you will send a resume and inform of your job search.

Name and business:	Contact information:

Draft an Email to Use Repeatedly When Sending a Resume

Draft a paragraph that you can use many times to introduce yourself to a new connection or a new contact to whom you are providing a resume:

_____

_____

_____

_____

_____

_____

_____

_____

_____

_____

_____

_____

_____

_____

Draft a Cover Letter

Draft a cover letter which you can use to apply to many positions. Make sure that you will only have to change a few sentences each time you send it to a new recipient.

Your name:

_____

Your address:

_____

Your telephone number:

_____

Your email address:

_____

Recipient's name and address:

_____

_____

_____

Dear _____,

_____

_____

_____

_____

_____

_____

_____

_____

_____

_____

_____

_____

_____

Sincerely,

Your signature:

_____

Your typed name:

_____

Revise Your Cover Letter

Revise your cover letter by creating a second draft. Make changes that you will be happy with.

Your name:

_____

Your address:

_____

Your telephone number:

_____

Your email address:

_____

Recipient's name and address:

_____

_____

_____

Dear _____,

_____

_____

_____

_____

_____

_____

_____

_____

_____

_____

_____

_____

_____

Sincerely,

Your signature:

_____

Your typed name:

_____

A Final Cover Letter

Revise your cover letter again, bringing it into final form. Make sure that you can use it to apply to many positions. You will only want to change a few sentences each time you send it to a new recipient.

Your name:

_____

Your address:

_____

Your telephone number:

_____

Your email address:

_____

Recipient's name and address:

_____

_____

_____

Dear _____,

_____

_____

_____

_____

_____

_____

_____

_____

_____

_____

_____

_____

_____

Sincerely,

Your signature:

_____

Your typed name:

_____

List Sources for Job Posts

Write a list of sources of job posts and the websites or other locations (for example, the library for trade publications) where you can find the sources later.

The Source:	Its Website or Location:

The Best Sources for Job Posts

Now, narrow down your list to the best sources which you plan to visit most often. Use this list frequently, and bring in your longer list as needed.

The Best Job Post Sources:	Their Websites or Locations:

List of Applications You Have Sent

Keep an electronic copy of your submissions and draft a list of positions to which you have applied. For each application you send, make the following notes.

Business name: _____

_____

_____

Position: _____

_____

_____

Date sent: _____

Resume version sent: _____

Person to whom you sent the application and his contact information: _____

_____

_____

_____

Response received: _____

_____

_____

_____

_____

Business name: _____

_____

_____

Position: _____

_____

_____

Date sent: _____

Resume version sent: _____

Person to whom you sent the application and his contact information: _____

_____

_____

_____

Response received: _____

_____

_____

_____

_____

_____

_____

Business name: _____

_____

_____

Position: _____

_____

_____

Date sent: _____

Resume version sent: _____

Person to whom you sent the application and his contact information: _____

_____

_____

_____

Response received: _____

_____

_____

_____

_____

_____

_____

Business name: _____

_____

_____

Position: _____

_____

_____

Date sent: _____

Resume version sent: _____

Person to whom you sent the application and his contact information: _____

_____

_____

_____

Response received: _____

_____

_____

_____

_____

_____

_____

Business name: _____

_____

_____

Position: _____

_____

_____

Date sent: _____

Resume version sent: _____

Person to whom you sent the application and his contact information: _____

_____

_____

_____

Response received: _____

_____

_____

_____

_____

_____

_____

Business name: _____

_____

_____

Position: _____

_____

_____

Date sent: _____

Resume version sent: _____

Person to whom you sent the application and his contact information: _____

_____

_____

_____

Response received: _____

_____

_____

_____

_____

_____

_____

Business name: _____

_____

_____

Position: _____

_____

_____

Date sent: _____

Resume version sent: _____

Person to whom you sent the application and his contact information: _____

_____

_____

_____

Response received: _____

_____

_____

_____

_____

_____

Business name: _____

_____

_____

Position: _____

_____

_____

Date sent: _____

Resume version sent: _____

Person to whom you sent the application and his contact information: _____

_____

_____

_____

Response received: _____

_____

_____

_____

_____

_____

_____

Business name: _____

_____

_____

Position: _____

_____

_____

Date sent: _____

Resume version sent: _____

Person to whom you sent the application and his contact information: _____

_____

_____

_____

Response received: _____

_____

_____

_____

_____

_____

_____

Business name: _____

_____

_____

Position: _____

_____

_____

Date sent: _____

Resume version sent: _____

Person to whom you sent the application and his contact information: _____

_____

_____

_____

Response received: _____

_____

_____

_____

_____

_____

_____

Business name: _____

_____

_____

Position: _____

_____

_____

Date sent: _____

Resume version sent: _____

Person to whom you sent the application and his contact information: _____

_____

_____

_____

Response received: _____

_____

_____

_____

_____

_____

_____

Business name: _____

_____

_____

Position: _____

_____

_____

Date sent: _____

Resume version sent: _____

Person to whom you sent the application and his contact information: _____

_____

_____

_____

Response received: _____

_____

_____

_____

_____

_____

_____

Business name: _____

_____

_____

Position: _____

_____

_____

Date sent: _____

Resume version sent: _____

Person to whom you sent the application and his contact information: _____

_____

_____

_____

Response received: _____

_____

_____

_____

_____

_____

_____

Business name: _____

_____

_____

Position: _____

_____

_____

Date sent: _____

Resume version sent: _____

Person to whom you sent the application and his contact information: _____

_____

_____

_____

Response received: _____

_____

_____

_____

_____

_____

_____

Business name: _____

_____

_____

Position: _____

_____

_____

Date sent: _____

Resume version sent: _____

Person to whom you sent the application and his contact information: _____

_____

_____

_____

Response received: _____

_____

_____

_____

_____

_____

_____

_____

Business name: _____

_____

_____

Position: _____

_____

_____

Date sent: _____

Resume version sent: _____

Person to whom you sent the application and his contact information: _____

_____

_____

_____

Response received: _____

_____

_____

_____

_____

_____

_____

Business name: _____

_____

_____

Position: _____

_____

_____

Date sent: _____

Resume version sent: _____

Person to whom you sent the application and his contact information: _____

_____

_____

_____

Response received: _____

_____

_____

_____

_____

_____

_____

Business name: _____

_____

_____

Position: _____

_____

_____

Date sent: _____

Resume version sent: _____

Person to whom you sent the application and his contact information: _____

_____

_____

_____

Response received: _____

_____

_____

_____

_____

_____

_____

Business name: _____

_____

_____

Position: _____

_____

_____

Date sent: _____

Resume version sent: _____

Person to whom you sent the application and his contact information: _____

_____

_____

_____

Response received: _____

_____

_____

_____

_____

_____

_____

Business name: _____

_____

_____

Position: _____

_____

_____

Date sent: _____

Resume version sent: _____

Person to whom you sent the application and his contact information: _____

_____

_____

_____

Response received: _____

_____

_____

_____

_____

_____

_____

THE "NO EXPERIENCE" JOB SEARCH: STRATEGY AND WORKBOOK

Business name: _____

_____

_____

Position: _____

_____

_____

Date sent: _____

Resume version sent: _____

Person to whom you sent the application and his contact information: _____

_____

_____

_____

Response received: _____

_____

_____

_____

_____

_____

_____

Business name: _____

_____

_____

Position: _____

_____

_____

Date sent: _____

Resume version sent: _____

Person to whom you sent the application and his contact information: _____

_____

_____

_____

Response received: _____

_____

_____

_____

_____

_____

_____

Business name: _____

_____

_____

Position: _____

_____

_____

Date sent: _____

Resume version sent: _____

Person to whom you sent the application and his contact information: _____

_____

_____

_____

Response received: _____

_____

_____

_____

_____

_____

_____

Business name: _____

_____

_____

Position: _____

_____

_____

Date sent: _____

Resume version sent: _____

Person to whom you sent the application and his contact information: _____

_____

_____

_____

Response received: _____

_____

_____

_____

_____

_____

_____

Business name: _____

_____

_____

Position: _____

_____

_____

Date sent: _____

Resume version sent: _____

Person to whom you sent the application and his contact information: _____

_____

_____

_____

Response received: _____

_____

_____

_____

_____

_____

_____

_____

Business name: _____

_____

_____

Position: _____

_____

_____

Date sent: _____

Resume version sent: _____

Person to whom you sent the application and his contact information: _____

_____

_____

_____

Response received: _____

_____

_____

_____

_____

_____

_____

Business name: _____

_____

_____

Position: _____

_____

_____

Date sent: _____

Resume version sent: _____

Person to whom you sent the application and his contact information: _____

_____

_____

_____

Response received: _____

_____

_____

_____

_____

_____

_____

Business name: _____

_____

_____

Position: _____

_____

_____

Date sent: _____

Resume version sent: _____

Person to whom you sent the application and his contact information: _____

_____

_____

_____

Response received: _____

_____

_____

_____

_____

_____

_____

Business name: _____

_____

_____

Position: _____

_____

_____

Date sent: _____

Resume version sent: _____

Person to whom you sent the application and his contact information: _____

_____

_____

_____

Response received: _____

_____

_____

_____

_____

_____

_____

Business name: _____

_____

_____

Position: _____

_____

_____

Date sent: _____

Resume version sent: _____

Person to whom you sent the application and his contact information: _____

_____

_____

_____

Response received: _____

_____

_____

_____

_____

_____

_____

_____

Table of Potential References to Use

Potential Reference's Name	How You Know Them	Reference's Email and Telephone	Date Requested and Response

A Full List of References

Draft a full list of references. Include those who have agreed to your request. You generally need three references for most positions. Write down the following information about your references, then type a final list of references.

First Reference

Name of reference: _____

_____

Reference's position and business or school: _____

_____

Relationship to you: _____

_____

Email address: _____

Telephone number: _____

Notes: _____

_____

Second Reference

Name of reference: _____

_____

Reference's position and business or school: _____

_____

Relationship to you: _____

_____

Email address: _____

Telephone number: _____

Notes: _____

_____

Third Reference

Name of reference: _____

_____

Reference's position and business or school: _____

_____

Relationship to you: _____

_____

Email address: _____

Telephone number: _____

Notes: _____

_____

Fourth Reference

Name of reference: _____

_____

Reference's position and business or school: _____

_____

Relationship to you: _____

_____

Email address: _____

Telephone number: _____

Notes: _____

_____

Fifth Reference

Name of reference: _____

_____

Reference's position and business or school: _____

_____

Relationship to you: _____

_____

Email address: _____

Telephone number: _____

Notes: _____

_____

Sixth Reference

Name of reference: _____

_____

Reference's position and business or school: _____

_____

Relationship to you: _____

_____

Email address: _____

Telephone number: _____

Notes: _____

_____

Plan How to Minimize "Bad Influences"

Develop a plan regarding how to shield future employers from being misinformed.

Consider whether you will provide a future employer with contact information for a prior boss who may be a "bad influence." Write down your conclusion here: _____

_____

_____

_____

_____

_____

_____

_____

Consider whether you will have future employers communicate only with your prior company's office of human resources. Write down your plan here: _____

_____

_____

_____

_____

_____

Consider whether you will have any communications with your prior boss if there is no office of human resources, your goal, and what you will say. Write down your plan here: _____

_____

_____

_____

_____

_____

_____

_____

_____

_____

_____

_____

_____

_____

_____

_____

_____

Write down your final decisions regarding shielding a future employer from being misinformed: _____

_____

_____

_____

_____

_____

_____

_____

_____

_____

_____

_____

_____

_____

_____

_____

_____

Explaining a Bad Ending to a Prior Position on an Interview

Next, create a plan for communicating about the end of your prior position in an interview for your next position.

Delineate the points that you might need to make if you are asked how the prior job ended (attempt to keep these very brief when spoken): _____

_____

_____

_____

_____

_____

_____

_____

_____

_____

_____

_____

_____

_____

Based on your explanation, the follow up questions that you might receive are: ___

_____

_____

_____

_____

_____

_____

_____

_____

_____

_____

You responses to these questions might be:

_____

_____

_____

_____

_____

_____

_____

_____

_____

_____

_____

_____

_____

_____

Finally, consider how you can transition the conversation back to your qualifications. For example, suggesting that the interviewer call one of the people on your list of references and providing this list to the interviewer such as by stating, "I can provide excellent references for my qualifications. Here is my list of references."

Write additional ideas for transitioning the conversation back to your qualifications:

_____

_____

_____

_____

_____

_____

_____

_____

_____

_____

_____

_____

_____

_____

Making Connections at Events

Write a list of places where you can meet people who work for the type of business to which you are applying. For example, continuing education classes in your field, courses for professional certification and re-certification, presentations and seminars on topics related to your profession, and conventions and exhibitions designed for job searching and networking.

-
-
-
-
-
-
-
-
-
-
-
-
-
-
-
-

Identify those in your area which you like the most, the dates, and any cost. Make a plan to attend one or two. Then, make sure to buy a ticket or reserve your spot.

Here is space for your list of opportunities in your area which you are most likely to attend.

Name and location: _____

Date: _____

Cost: _____

Name and location: _____

Date: _____

Cost: _____

Name and location: _____

Date: _____

Cost: _____

Name and location: _____

Date: _____

Cost: _____

Strategic Networking

When you attend an event you have chosen to make connections, obtain the business cards of everyone you meet and make a note regarding all of the positive things they say about the business for which they work. For example, send yourself an email or text with a note right after each conversation so you will not forget names and statements made by those new connections. Then, write them down here when you get home.

Name and position: _____

Business name and location: _____

What she said that is positive about the business: _____

_____

_____

_____

_____

_____

_____

_____

List any open positions in this business which you find online and for which you would like to apply: _____

_____

_____

_____

_____

Send an application and then note the date and to whom you applied: _____

_____

_____

_____

_____

List the person to whom you will send your networking letter via email (find a person in the company who you might work with based on the job description, and then send the letter to that person): _____

_____

_____

_____

Once you send your networking letter, make a note regarding when it was sent and the resume version that you enclosed: _____

_____

_____

_____

Make a note of any responses which you receive and all follow up communications:

_____

_____

_____

_____

_____

_____

_____

_____

_____

_____

_____

_____

_____

_____

Name and position: _____

Business name and location: _____

What she said that is positive about the business: _____

_____

_____

_____

_____

_____

_____

_____

List any open positions in this business which you find online and for which you would like to apply: _____

_____

_____

_____

_____

_____

_____

Send an application and then note the date and to whom you applied: _____

_____

_____

_____

_____

_____

List the person to whom you will send your networking letter via email (find a person in the company who you might work with based on the job description, and then send the letter to that person): _____

_____

_____

_____

_____

Once you send your networking letter, make a note regarding when it was sent and the resume version that you enclosed: _____

_____

_____

_____

Make a note of any responses which you receive and all follow up communications:

_____

_____

_____

_____

_____

_____

_____

_____

_____

_____

_____

_____

_____

_____

Name and position: _____

Business name and location: _____

What she said that is positive about the business: _____

_____

_____

_____

_____

_____

_____

_____

List any open positions in this business which you find online and for which you would like to apply: _____

_____

_____

_____

_____

_____

_____

Send an application and then note the date and to whom you applied: _____

_____

_____

_____

_____

_____

List the person to whom you will send your networking letter via email (find a person in the company who you might work with based on the job description, and then send the letter to that person): _____

_____

_____

_____

Once you send your networking letter, make a note regarding when it was sent and the resume version that you enclosed: _____

_____

_____

_____

_____

_____

Make a note of any responses which you receive and all follow up communications:

_____

_____

_____

_____

_____

_____

_____

_____

_____

_____

_____

_____

_____

_____

Name and position: _____

Business name and location: _____

What she said that is positive about the business: _____

_____

_____

_____

_____

_____

_____

_____

List any open positions in this business which you find online and for which you would like to apply: _____

_____

_____

_____

_____

_____

Send an application and then note the date and to whom you applied: _____

_____

_____

_____

_____

_____

List the person to whom you will send your networking letter via email (find a person in the company who you might work with based on the job description, and then send the letter to that person): _____

_____

_____

_____

_____

Once you send your networking letter, make a note regarding when it was sent and the resume version that you enclosed: _____

_____

_____

_____

_____

_____

Make a note of any responses which you receive and all follow up communications:

_____

_____

_____

_____

_____

_____

_____

_____

_____

_____

_____

_____

_____

_____

_____

Name and position: _____

Business name and location: _____

What she said that is positive about the business: _____

_____

_____

_____

_____

_____

_____

_____

List any open positions in this business which you find online and for which you would like to apply: _____

_____

_____

_____

_____

_____

Send an application and then note the date and to whom you applied: _____

_____

_____

_____

_____

_____

List the person to whom you will send your networking letter via email (find a person in the company who you might work with based on the job description, and then send the letter to that person): _____

_____

_____

_____

_____

Once you send your networking letter, make a note regarding when it was sent and the resume version that you enclosed: _____

_____

_____

_____

_____

_____

Make a note of any responses which you receive and all follow up communications:

_____

_____

_____

_____

_____

_____

_____

_____

_____

_____

_____

_____

_____

_____

Name and position: _____

Business name and location: _____

What she said that is positive about the business: _____

_____

_____

_____

_____

_____

_____

_____

List any open positions in this business which you find online and for which you would like to apply: _____

_____

_____

_____

_____

_____

_____

Send an application and then note the date and to whom you applied: _____

_____

_____

_____

_____

List the person to whom you will send your networking letter via email (find a person in the company who you might work with based on the job description, and then send the letter to that person): _____

_____

_____

_____

Once you send your networking letter, make a note regarding when it was sent and the resume version that you enclosed: _____

_____

_____

_____

_____

_____

Make a note of any responses which you receive and all follow up communications:

_____

_____

_____

_____

_____

_____

_____

_____

_____

_____

_____

_____

_____

Name and position: _____

Business name and location: _____

What she said that is positive about the business: _____

_____

_____

_____

_____

_____

_____

_____

List any open positions in this business which you find online and for which you would like to apply: _____

_____

_____

_____

_____

_____

_____

_____

Send an application and then note the date and to whom you applied: _____

_____

_____

_____

_____

List the person to whom you will send your networking letter via email (find a person in the company who you might work with based on the job description, and then send the letter to that person): _____

_____

_____

_____

Once you send your networking letter, make a note regarding when it was sent and the resume version that you enclosed: _____

_____

_____

_____

_____

_____

Make a note of any responses which you receive and all follow up communications:

_____

_____

_____

_____

_____

_____

_____

_____

_____

_____

_____

_____

Interview Preparation Checklist

First checklist

Interview date: _____

Business name and location: _____

Position: _____

_____

_____

_____

Check off the documents you will bring with you, once they are in a portfolio:

☐ Resume (this should be the same version which you used to apply)

☐ References list

☐ School transcript (order a non-official transcript and have it emailed or mailed to you)

☐ Writing sample (or other sample of work which is usual in your field)

☐ _____

☐ _____

☐ _____

Also, consider how long it will take you to get there and look up directions. Finally, determine what you will wear and have it ready.

If you are nervous and have time before the interview, then go over these things again. Re-review the company website and the job posting and make notes for the interview: _____

_____

_____

_____

_____

_____

_____

_____

_____

Re-review your master resume list and practice explaining your qualifications ("I know that I can do this because I once…" or "I have this skill as shown by my coursework in…"): _____

_____

_____

_____

_____

_____

_____

_____

_____

Additional checklist

Interview date: _____

Business name and location: _____

Position: _____

_____

_____

_____

Check off the documents you will bring with you, once they are in a portfolio:

- ☐ Resume (this should be the same version which you used to apply)
- ☐ References list
- ☐ School transcript (order a non-official transcript and have it emailed or mailed to you)
- ☐ Writing sample (or other sample of work which is usual in your field)
- ☐ _____
- ☐ _____
- ☐ _____

Also, consider how long it will take you to get there and look up directions. Finally, determine what you will wear and have it ready.

If you are nervous and have time before the interview, then go over these things again. Re-review the company website and the job posting and make notes for the interview: _____

_____

_____

_____

_____

_____

_____

_____

_____

_____

_____

Re-review your master resume list and practice explaining your qualifications ("I know that I can do this because I once…" or "I have this skill as shown by my coursework in…"): _____

_____

_____

_____

_____

_____

_____

_____

_____

Additional checklist

Interview date: _____

Business name and location: _____

Position: _____

_____

_____

_____

Check off the documents you will bring with you, once they are in a portfolio:

- ☐ Resume (this should be the same version which you used to apply)
- ☐ References list
- ☐ School transcript (order a non-official transcript and have it emailed or mailed to you)
- ☐ Writing sample (or other sample of work which is usual in your field)
- ☐ _____
- ☐ _____
- ☐ _____

Also, consider how long it will take you to get there and look up directions. Finally, determine what you will wear and have it ready.

If you are nervous and have time before the interview, then go over these things again. Re-review the company website and the job posting and make notes for the interview: _____

_____

_____

_____

_____

_____

_____

_____

_____

_____

_____

Re-review your master resume list and practice explaining your qualifications ("I know that I can do this because I once…" or "I have this skill as shown by my coursework in…"): _____

_____

_____

_____

_____

_____

_____

_____

Additional checklist

Interview date: _____

Business name and location: _____

Position: _____

_____

_____

_____

Check off the documents you will bring with you, once they are in a portfolio:

- ☐ Resume (this should be the same version which you used to apply)
- ☐ References list
- ☐ School transcript (order a non-official transcript and have it emailed or mailed to you)
- ☐ Writing sample (or other sample of work which is usual in your field)
- ☐ _____
- ☐ _____
- ☐ _____

Also, consider how long it will take you to get there and look up directions. Finally, determine what you will wear and have it ready.

If you are nervous and have time before the interview, then go over these things again. Re-review the company website and the job posting and make notes for the interview: _____

_____

_____

_____

_____

_____

_____

_____

_____

_____

_____

Re-review your master resume list and practice explaining your qualifications ("I know that I can do this because I once…" or "I have this skill as shown by my coursework in…"): _____

_____

_____

_____

_____

_____

_____

_____

_____

Additional checklist

Interview date: _____

Business name and location: _____

Position: _____

_____

_____

_____

Check off the documents you will bring with you, once they are in a portfolio:

☐ Resume (this should be the same version which you used to apply)

☐ References list

☐ School transcript (order a non-official transcript and have it emailed or mailed to you)

☐ Writing sample (or other sample of work which is usual in your field)

☐ _____

☐ _____

☐ _____

Also, consider how long it will take you to get there and look up directions. Finally, determine what you will wear and have it ready.

If you are nervous and have time before the interview, then go over these things again. Re-review the company website and the job posting and make notes for the interview: _____

_____

_____

_____

_____

_____

_____

_____

_____

_____

_____

_____

Re-review your master resume list and practice explaining your qualifications ("I know that I can do this because I once…" or "I have this skill as shown by my coursework in…"): _____

_____

_____

_____

_____

_____

_____

_____

_____

Additional checklist

Interview date: _____

Business name and location: _____

Position: _____

_____

_____

_____

Check off the documents you will bring with you, once they are in a portfolio:

- ☐ Resume (this should be the same version which you used to apply)
- ☐ References list
- ☐ School transcript (order a non-official transcript and have it emailed or mailed to you)
- ☐ Writing sample (or other sample of work which is usual in your field)
- ☐ _____
- ☐ _____
- ☐ _____

Also, consider how long it will take you to get there and look up directions. Finally, determine what you will wear and have it ready.

If you are nervous and have time before the interview, then go over these things again. Re-review the company website and the job posting and make notes for the interview: _____

_____

_____

_____

_____

_____

_____

_____

_____

_____

_____

Re-review your master resume list and practice explaining your qualifications ("I know that I can do this because I once…" or "I have this skill as shown by my coursework in…"): _____

_____

_____

_____

_____

_____

_____

_____

Additional checklist

Interview date: _____

Business name and location: _____

Position: _____

_____

_____

_____

Check off the documents you will bring with you, once they are in a portfolio:

☐ Resume (this should be the same version which you used to apply)

☐ References list

☐ School transcript (order a non-official transcript and have it emailed or mailed to you)

☐ Writing sample (or other sample of work which is usual in your field)

☐ _____

☐ _____

☐ _____

Also, consider how long it will take you to get there and look up directions. Finally, determine what you will wear and have it ready.

If you are nervous and have time before the interview, then go over these things again. Re-review the company website and the job posting and make notes for the interview: _____

_____

_____

_____

_____

_____

_____

_____

_____

_____

_____

Re-review your master resume list and practice explaining your qualifications ("I know that I can do this because I once…" or "I have this skill as shown by my coursework in…"): _____

_____

_____

_____

_____

_____

_____

_____

_____

Fully Prepare for Your Interview

Practice Interviewing For One Position:

First, prepare to discuss coursework qualifications: Consider how to discuss your coursework qualifications in an interview setting. Do this by explaining what you know you are qualified to do and how the coursework prepared you. Practice making the following statements.

I can: _____

_____

_____

_____

_____

_____

_____

_____

I gained this skill (or learned this skill) when: _____

_____

_____

_____

_____

_____

_____

_____

_____

I demonstrated my skills, which qualify me to work for you, by passing these tests:

_____

_____

_____

_____

_____

_____

_____

I am ready to apply this skill in a company environment because:

_____

_____

_____

_____

_____

_____

_____

_____

Remember to prepare to handle any question or negativity by an interviewer: if it is suggested that coursework is not relevant experience, be ready to positively communicate that you have the skills needed to perform this particular job well. Fill in the table below (for help, use example statements from Chapter #2, Part Three: Explaining that Coursework is Experience to a Potential Employer).

An interviewer might argue that coursework is not relevant experience. He might say:	My response will be that I have the skills needed to perform the job well. I will say:

Next, practice describing single experiences to show that you are good at doing something which you have only done once. These are going to be your oral descriptions, so write them in the way in which you will practice saying them.

Describe a single experience:

_____

_____

_____

_____

_____

_____

_____

Now, explain how it shows that you can do a necessary task for the job you seek:

_____

_____

_____

_____

_____

_____

_____

Also, practice describing skills from unrelated part-time work: practice describing any skill that is needed in the position you seek which you gained from a dissimilar part-time job. Pretend that you are in an interview setting as you prepare what you will say.

The skill needed by the employer is: _____

_____

_____

_____

_____

Describe what you can do based on your part-time experience: _____

_____

_____

_____

_____

_____

_____

_____

_____

_____

Explain that you are qualified to perform the skill needed by the employer: _____

_____

_____

_____

_____

_____

_____

_____

_____

Finally, practice describing and explaining all of your additional qualifications. Consider how to communicate why you know that you can do each item which you have listed on your resume. Try to consider the questions an interviewer might ask and how you will respond as you work through your explanations.

You are qualified to: _____

_____

_____

_____

_____

_____

Describe what you can do:

_____

_____

_____

_____

_____

_____

_____

Explain why you know you can do it:

_____

_____

_____

_____

_____

_____

_____

_____

_____

You are qualified to: _____

_____

_____

_____

_____

_____

Describe what you can do:

_____

_____

_____

_____

_____

_____

_____

_____

Explain why you know you can do it:

_____

_____

_____

_____

_____

_____

_____

_____

_____

_____

_____

Practice Interviewing For a Different Position

First, prepare to discuss coursework qualifications: Consider how to discuss your coursework qualifications in an interview setting. Do this by explaining what you know you are qualified to do and how the coursework prepared you. Practice making the following statements.

I can: _____

_____

_____

_____

_____

_____

_____

_____

I gained this skill (or learned this skill) when: _____

_____

_____

_____

_____

_____

I demonstrated my skills, which qualify me to work for you, by passing these tests:

_____

_____

_____

_____

_____

_____

_____

I am ready to apply this skill in a company environment because:

_____

_____

_____

_____

_____

_____

_____

_____

Remember to prepare to handle any question or negativity by an interviewer: if it is suggested that coursework is not relevant experience, be ready to positively communicate that you have the skills needed to perform this particular job well. Fill in the table below (for help, use example statements from Chapter #2, Part Three: Explaining that Coursework is Experience to a Potential Employer).

An interviewer might argue that coursework is not relevant experience. He might say:	My response will be that I have the skills needed to perform the job well. I will say:

Next, practice describing single experiences to show that you are good at doing something which you have only done once. These are going to be your oral descriptions, so write them in the way in which you will practice saying them.

Describe a single experience:

_____

_____

_____

_____

_____

_____

_____

_____

Now, explain how it shows that you can do a necessary task for the job you seek:

_____

_____

_____

_____

_____

_____

Also, practice describing skills from unrelated part-time work: practice describing any skill that is needed in the position you seek which you gained from a dissimilar part-time job. Pretend that you are in an interview setting as you prepare what you will say.

The skill needed by the employer is: _____

_____

_____

_____

_____

Describe what you can do based on your part-time experience: _____

_____

_____

_____

_____

_____

_____

_____

_____

_____

Explain that you are qualified to perform the skill needed by the employer: _____

_____

_____

_____

_____

_____

_____

_____

_____

_____

Finally, practice describing and explaining all of your additional qualifications. Consider how to communicate why you know that you can do each item which you have listed on your resume. Try to consider the questions an interviewer might ask and how you will respond as you work through your explanations.

You are qualified to: _____

_____

_____

_____

_____

_____

Describe what you can do:
_____

_____

_____

_____

_____

_____

_____

_____

_____

Explain why you know you can do it:

_____

_____

_____

_____

_____

_____

_____

_____

You are qualified to: _____

_____

_____

_____

_____

Describe what you can do:

_____

_____

_____

_____

_____

_____

_____

_____

Explain why you know you can do it:

_____

_____

_____

_____

_____

_____

_____

_____

_____

_____

Practice Interviewing For a Different Position

First, prepare to discuss coursework qualifications: Consider how to discuss your coursework qualifications in an interview setting. Do this by explaining what you know you are qualified to do and how the coursework prepared you. Practice making the following statements.

I can: _____

_____

_____

_____

_____

_____

_____

_____

I gained this skill (or learned this skill) when: _____

_____

_____

_____

_____

I demonstrated my skills, which qualify me to work for you, by passing these tests:

_____

_____

_____

_____

_____

_____

_____

_____

I am ready to apply this skill in a company environment because:

_____

_____

_____

_____

_____

_____

_____

_____

Remember to prepare to handle any question or negativity by an interviewer: if it is suggested that coursework is not relevant experience, be ready to positively communicate that you have the skills needed to perform this particular job well. Fill in the table below (for help, use example statements from Chapter #2, Part Three: Explaining that Coursework is Experience to a Potential Employer).

An interviewer might argue that coursework is not relevant experience. He might say:	My response will be that I have the skills needed to perform the job well. I will say:

Next, practice describing single experiences to show that you are good at doing something which you have only done once. These are going to be your oral descriptions, so write them in the way in which you will practice saying them.

Describe a single experience:

_____

_____

_____

_____

_____

_____

_____

_____

_____

Now, explain how it shows that you can do a necessary task for the job you seek:

_____

_____

_____

_____

_____

_____

_____

Also, practice describing skills from unrelated part-time work: practice describing any skill that is needed in the position you seek which you gained from a dissimilar part-time job. Pretend that you are in an interview setting as you prepare what you will say.

The skill needed by the employer is: _____

_____

_____

_____

_____

Describe what you can do based on your part-time experience: _____

_____

_____

_____

_____

_____

_____

_____

_____

_____

_____

Explain that you are qualified to perform the skill needed by the employer: _____

_____

_____

_____

_____

_____

_____

_____

_____

_____

Finally, practice describing and explaining all of your additional qualifications. Consider how to communicate why you know that you can do each item which you have listed on your resume. Try to consider the questions an interviewer might ask and how you will respond as you work through your explanations.

You are qualified to: _____

_____

_____

_____

_____

_____

Describe what you can do:

_____

_____

_____

_____

_____

_____

_____

_____

_____

Explain why you know you can do it:

_____

_____

_____

_____

_____

_____

_____

_____

You are qualified to: _____

_____

_____

_____

_____

Describe what you can do:

_____

_____

_____

_____

_____

_____

_____

Explain why you know you can do it:

_____

_____

_____

_____

_____

_____

_____

_____

_____

Practice Interviewing For a Different Position

First, prepare to discuss coursework qualifications: Consider how to discuss your coursework qualifications in an interview setting. Do this by explaining what you know you are qualified to do and how the coursework prepared you. Practice making the following statements.

I can: _____

_____

_____

_____

_____

_____

_____

_____

I gained this skill (or learned this skill) when: _____

_____

_____

_____

_____

I demonstrated my skills, which qualify me to work for you, by passing these tests:

_____

_____

_____

_____

_____

_____

I am ready to apply this skill in a company environment because:

_____

_____

_____

_____

_____

_____

_____

Remember to prepare to handle any question or negativity by an interviewer: if it is suggested that coursework is not relevant experience, be ready to positively communicate that you have the skills needed to perform this particular job well. Fill in the table below (for help, use example statements from Chapter #2, Part Three: Explaining that Coursework is Experience to a Potential Employer).

An interviewer might argue that coursework is not relevant experience. He might say:	My response will be that I have the skills needed to perform the job well. I will say:

Next, practice describing single experiences to show that you are good at doing something which you have only done once. These are going to be your oral descriptions, so write them in the way in which you will practice saying them.

Describe a single experience:

_____

_____

_____

_____

_____

_____

_____

_____

Now, explain how it shows that you can do a necessary task for the job you seek:

_____

_____

_____

_____

_____

_____

Also, practice describing skills from unrelated part-time work: practice describing any skill that is needed in the position you seek which you gained from a dissimilar part-time job. Pretend that you are in an interview setting as you prepare what you will say.

The skill needed by the employer is: _____

_____

_____

_____

_____

Describe what you can do based on your part-time experience: _____

_____

_____

_____

_____

_____

_____

_____

_____

Explain that you are qualified to perform the skill needed by the employer: _____

_____

_____

_____

_____

_____

_____

_____

_____

_____

Finally, practice describing and explaining all of your additional qualifications. Consider how to communicate why you know that you can do each item which you have listed on your resume. Try to consider the questions an interviewer might ask and how you will respond as you work through your explanations.

You are qualified to: _____

_____

_____

_____

_____

Describe what you can do:

_____

_____

_____

_____

_____

_____

_____

_____

_____

Explain why you know you can do it:

_____

_____

_____

_____

_____

_____

_____

You are qualified to: _____

_____

_____

_____

_____

Describe what you can do:

_____

_____

_____

_____

_____

_____

_____

_____

Explain why you know you can do it:

_____

_____

_____

_____

_____

_____

_____

_____

_____

Practice Interviewing For a Different Position

First, prepare to discuss coursework qualifications: Consider how to discuss your coursework qualifications in an interview setting. Do this by explaining what you know you are qualified to do and how the coursework prepared you. Practice making the following statements.

I can: _____

_____

_____

_____

_____

_____

_____

_____

I gained this skill (or learned this skill) when: _____

_____

_____

_____

_____

_____

I demonstrated my skills, which qualify me to work for you, by passing these tests:

_____

_____

_____

_____

_____

_____

_____

I am ready to apply this skill in a company environment because:

_____

_____

_____

_____

_____

_____

_____

Remember to prepare to handle any question or negativity by an interviewer: if it is suggested that coursework is not relevant experience, be ready to positively communicate that you have the skills needed to perform this particular job well. Fill in the table below (for help, use example statements from Chapter #2, Part Three: Explaining that Coursework is Experience to a Potential Employer).

An interviewer might argue that coursework is not relevant experience. He might say:	My response will be that I have the skills needed to perform the job well. I will say:

Next, practice describing single experiences to show that you are good at doing something which you have only done once. These are going to be your oral descriptions, so write them in the way in which you will practice saying them.

Describe a single experience:

_____

_____

_____

_____

_____

_____

_____

_____

Now, explain how it shows that you can do a necessary task for the job you seek:

_____

_____

_____

_____

_____

_____

Also, practice describing skills from unrelated part-time work: practice describing any skill that is needed in the position you seek which you gained from a dissimilar part-time job. Pretend that you are in an interview setting as you prepare what you will say.

The skill needed by the employer is: _____

_____

_____

_____

_____

Describe what you can do based on your part-time experience: _____

_____

_____

_____

_____

_____

_____

_____

_____

_____

Explain that you are qualified to perform the skill needed by the employer: _____

_____

_____

_____

_____

_____

_____

_____

_____

Finally, practice describing and explaining all of your additional qualifications. Consider how to communicate why you know that you can do each item which you have listed on your resume. Try to consider the questions an interviewer might ask and how you will respond as you work through your explanations.

You are qualified to: _____

_____

_____

_____

_____

_____

Describe what you can do:

_____

_____

_____

_____

_____

_____

_____

_____

_____

Explain why you know you can do it:

_____

_____

_____

_____

_____

_____

_____

_____

You are qualified to: _____

_____

_____

_____

_____

Describe what you can do:

_____

_____

_____

_____

_____

_____

_____

Explain why you know you can do it:

_____

_____

_____

_____

_____

_____

_____

_____

Practice Interviewing For a Different Position

First, prepare to discuss coursework qualifications: Consider how to discuss your coursework qualifications in an interview setting. Do this by explaining what you know you are qualified to do and how the coursework prepared you. Practice making the following statements.

I can: _____

_____

_____

_____

_____

_____

_____

_____

I gained this skill (or learned this skill) when: _____

_____

_____

_____

_____

I demonstrated my skills, which qualify me to work for you, by passing these tests:

_____

_____

_____

_____

_____

_____

_____

I am ready to apply this skill in a company environment because:

_____

_____

_____

_____

_____

_____

_____

_____

Remember to prepare to handle any question or negativity by an interviewer: if it is suggested that coursework is not relevant experience, be ready to positively communicate that you have the skills needed to perform this particular job well. Fill in the table below (for help, use example statements from Chapter #2, Part Three: Explaining that Coursework is Experience to a Potential Employer).

An interviewer might argue that coursework is not relevant experience. He might say:	My response will be that I have the skills needed to perform the job well. I will say:

Next, practice describing single experiences to show that you are good at doing something which you have only done once. These are going to be your oral descriptions, so write them in the way in which you will practice saying them.

Describe a single experience:

_____

_____

_____

_____

_____

_____

_____

_____

Now, explain how it shows that you can do a necessary task for the job you seek:

_____

_____

_____

_____

_____

_____

_____

Also, practice describing skills from unrelated part-time work: practice describing any skill that is needed in the position you seek which you gained from a dissimilar part-time job. Pretend that you are in an interview setting as you prepare what you will say.

The skill needed by the employer is: _____

_____

_____

_____

_____

Describe what you can do based on your part-time experience: _____

_____

_____

_____

_____

_____

_____

_____

_____

Explain that you are qualified to perform the skill needed by the employer: _____

_____

_____

_____

_____

_____

_____

_____

_____

_____

Finally, practice describing and explaining all of your additional qualifications. Consider how to communicate why you know that you can do each item which you have listed on your resume. Try to consider the questions an interviewer might ask and how you will respond as you work through your explanations.

You are qualified to: _____

_____

_____

_____

_____

_____

Describe what you can do:

_____

_____

_____

_____

_____

_____

_____

_____

_____

Explain why you know you can do it:

_____

_____

_____

_____

_____

_____

_____

You are qualified to: _____

_____

_____

_____

_____

Describe what you can do:

_____

_____

_____

_____

_____

_____

_____

Explain why you know you can do it:

_____

_____

_____

_____

_____

_____

_____

_____

_____

Consider the Position and Negotiate the Salary

After One Interview

After your interview, consider the position and prepare to negotiate the salary if the position is offered. Consider the following when thinking through what your decision will be and what you believe the compensation should be for the position.

List the things you like, and those things you dislike about the position, especially those things which you will be doing on a daily basis for this business:

-
-
-
-
-
-
-
-
-
-

List the things you like, and those things you dislike about this business:

-
-
-
-
-
-

Consider whether you like the office space, especially where you think you will be working (your desk space or office, if you have seen the area in which you might be located). Write down the things you like, and those things you dislike about this space: _____

_____

_____

_____

_____

_____

_____

_____

Do you think that you will work with any of the people you met on the interview and if so, would you like to work with them regularly? _____

_____

_____

_____

_____

_____

_____

What are the hours you will likely work if you are offered and you accept the position? Also, what will the commute be like for you?

Monday: _____

Tuesday: _____

Wednesday: _____

Thursday: _____

Friday: _____

Saturday: _____

Sunday: _____

Notes on the commute: _____

_____

_____

_____

_____

Overall, how do you feel about accepting this position if it is offered to you?

_____

_____

_____

_____

_____

_____

What salaries do you think others make in this position for this type of business? Add in any examples that you know of or which you find online and think could be accurate.

_____

_____

_____

_____

_____

Finally, determine the amount that you want to make for this business in this position. A salary range is a good way to conceptualize the lowest amount which you will accept, and the most which you can realistically hope to obtain.

_____

_____

_____

_____

_____

_____

_____

_____

_____

After Another Interview

After your interview, consider the position and prepare to negotiate the salary if the position is offered. Consider the following when thinking through what your decision will be and what you believe the compensation should be for the position.

List the things you like, and those things you dislike about the position, especially those things which you will be doing on a daily basis for this business:

-
-
-
-
-
-
-
-
-
-

List the things you like, and those things you dislike about this business:

-
-
-
-
-
-

Consider whether you like the office space, especially where you think you will be working (your desk space or office, if you have seen the area in which you might be located). Write down the things you like, and those things you dislike about this space: _____

_____

_____

_____

_____

_____

_____

_____

_____

Do you think that you will work with any of the people you met on the interview and if so, would you like to work with them regularly? _____

_____

_____

_____

_____

_____

_____

_____

What are the hours you will likely work if you are offered and you accept the position? Also, what will the commute be like for you?

Monday: _____

Tuesday: _____

Wednesday: _____

Thursday: _____

Friday: _____

Saturday: _____

Sunday: _____

Notes on the commute: _____

_____

_____

_____

_____

Overall, how do you feel about accepting this position if it is offered to you?

_____

_____

_____

_____

_____

_____

What salaries do you think others make in this position for this type of business? Add in any examples that you know of or which you find online and think could be accurate.

_____

_____

_____

_____

_____

Finally, determine the amount that you want to make for this business in this position. A salary range is a good way to conceptualize the lowest amount which you will accept, and the most which you can realistically hope to obtain.

_____

_____

_____

_____

_____

_____

_____

_____

_____

_____

After Another Interview

After your interview, consider the position and prepare to negotiate the salary if the position is offered. Consider the following when thinking through what your decision will be and what you believe the compensation should be for the position.

List the things you like, and those things you dislike about the position, especially those things which you will be doing on a daily basis for this business:

-
-
-
-
-
-
-
-
-
-
-

List the things you like, and those things you dislike about this business:

-
-
-
-
-
-

Consider whether you like the office space, especially where you think you will be working (your desk space or office, if you have seen the area in which you might be located). Write down the things you like, and those things you dislike about this space: _____

_____

_____

_____

_____

_____

_____

_____

_____

Do you think that you will work with any of the people you met on the interview and if so, would you like to work with them regularly? _____

_____

_____

_____

_____

_____

_____

_____

What are the hours you will likely work if you are offered and you accept the position? Also, what will the commute be like for you?

Monday: _____

Tuesday: _____

Wednesday: _____

Thursday: _____

Friday: _____

Saturday: _____

Sunday: _____

Notes on the commute: _____

_____

_____

_____

_____

Overall, how do you feel about accepting this position if it is offered to you?

_____

_____

_____

_____

_____

_____

What salaries do you think others make in this position for this type of business? Add in any examples that you know of or which you find online and think could be accurate.

_____

_____

_____

_____

_____

Finally, determine the amount that you want to make for this business in this position. A salary range is a good way to conceptualize the lowest amount which you will accept, and the most which you can realistically hope to obtain.

_____

_____

_____

_____

_____

_____

_____

_____

_____

_____

After Another Interview

After your interview, consider the position and prepare to negotiate the salary if the position is offered. Consider the following when thinking through what your decision will be and what you believe the compensation should be for the position.

List the things you like, and those things you dislike about the position, especially those things which you will be doing on a daily basis for this business:

-
-
-
-
-
-
-
-
-
-

List the things you like, and those things you dislike about this business:

-
-
-
-
-
-

Consider whether you like the office space, especially where you think you will be working (your desk space or office, if you have seen the area in which you might be located). Write down the things you like, and those things you dislike about this space: _____

_____

_____

_____

_____

_____

_____

_____

Do you think that you will work with any of the people you met on the interview and if so, would you like to work with them regularly? _____

_____

_____

_____

_____

_____

_____

_____

What are the hours you will likely work if you are offered and you accept the position? Also, what will the commute be like for you?

Monday: _____

Tuesday: _____

Wednesday: _____

Thursday: _____

Friday: _____

Saturday: _____

Sunday: _____

Notes on the commute: _____

_____

_____

_____

_____

Overall, how do you feel about accepting this position if it is offered to you?

_____

_____

_____

_____

_____

_____

What salaries do you think others make in this position for this type of business? Add in any examples that you know of or which you find online and think could be accurate.

_____

_____

_____

_____

_____

Finally, determine the amount that you want to make for this business in this position. A salary range is a good way to conceptualize the lowest amount which you will accept, and the most which you can realistically hope to obtain.

_____

_____

_____

_____

_____

_____

_____

_____

_____

_____

After Another Interview

After your interview, consider the position and prepare to negotiate the salary if the position is offered. Consider the following when thinking through what your decision will be and what you believe the compensation should be for the position.

List the things you like, and those things you dislike about the position, especially those things which you will be doing on a daily basis for this business:

-
-
-
-
-
-
-
-
-
-

List the things you like, and those things you dislike about this business:

-
-
-
-
-
-

Consider whether you like the office space, especially where you think you will be working (your desk space or office, if you have seen the area in which you might be located). Write down the things you like, and those things you dislike about this space: _____

_____

_____

_____

_____

_____

_____

_____

Do you think that you will work with any of the people you met on the interview and if so, would you like to work with them regularly? _____

_____

_____

_____

_____

_____

_____

What are the hours you will likely work if you are offered and you accept the position? Also, what will the commute be like for you?

Monday: _____

Tuesday: _____

Wednesday: _____

Thursday: _____

Friday: _____

Saturday: _____

Sunday: _____

Notes on the commute: _____

_____

_____

_____

_____

Overall, how do you feel about accepting this position if it is offered to you?

_____

_____

_____

_____

_____

_____

What salaries do you think others make in this position for this type of business? Add in any examples that you know of or which you find online and think could be accurate.

_____

_____

_____

_____

_____

Finally, determine the amount that you want to make for this business in this position. A salary range is a good way to conceptualize the lowest amount which you will accept, and the most which you can realistically hope to obtain.

_____

_____

_____

_____

_____

_____

_____

_____

_____

_____

www.ingramcontent.com/pod-product-compliance
Lightning Source LLC
Chambersburg PA
CBHW081412270326
41931CB00015B/3245